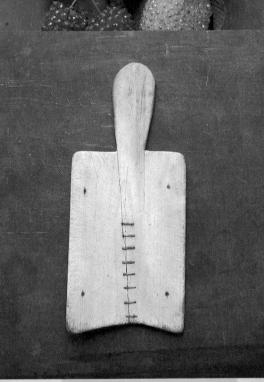

COLLECTED

COLLECTED

LIVING WITH THE THINGS YOU LOVE

FRITZ KARCH

AND

REBECCA
ROBERTSON

WITH

JEN RENZI

NEW PHOTOGRAPHY BY
DANA GALLAGHER

ABRAMS, NEW YORK

the CONTENTS

As style editors immersed in the world of collecting—and as lifelong members of the tribe ourselves—we have been privy to some of the most intriguing assemblages of ceramics, textiles, and glass. We've had the honor of visiting connoisseurs of all stripes to learn about their passions, and how they live with them.

What we discovered, surprisingly, was that most owners of incredible collections don't live in a manner that best showcases their assortments. Many keep their prized possessions stashed in drawers or closets or otherwise tucked away, troves of mod vintage napkins or chenille bedspreads are kept neatly folded in the linen cabinet, and mid-century ceramic vessels are grouped unceremoniously on a side table. The good silverware and place settings are only brought out

An enthusiast's decor typically mirrors his or her collecting sensibility. For this collector, CARVED CAMEO SHELLS are examples of the high level of refinement found in nature—a quality that also distinguishes the elegantly attenuated African porcupine quills used as bouquets. He is attentive to finish; hence the sophisticated interplay between the matteness of the shells and marble tabletop and the reflectivity of the glass. Even the wall color is just so: the perfect neutral gray to draw out the veins in the marble and the muted gilt-work.

for special occasions. Aesthetes attuned to subtleties of patina and finish aren't always able to translate that sensibility to the larger scale of a room's decor. And the most serious, curatorially minded collectors don't generally dwell with their treasures; they safeguard them in archival storage or safe-deposit boxes. That these wonderful collections, which bring so much delight to their owners, were not displayed to fullest effect felt like such a missed opportunity.

Over the years, we've grown increasingly impassioned to help our fellow enthusiasts live harmoniously with their collections. It's been our personal and professional mission to get treasures out of boxes and into their owners' daily surroundings: to hang antique copper food molds on the wall; to arrange tchotchkes by color palette; to exploit organizing devices like shelves, serving trays, and cabinets; and to revivify snuffboxes, pap boats, and other obsolete objects as artful vessels for flowers or spare change. Our experience styling magazine shoots and residential interiors (not to mention our own abodes) taught us a host of tips, tricks, and strategies for arranging multiples, composing tablescapes, and comingling objets d'art with intriguing oddities.

We yearned for a forum to relate these design methods to a wider audience. To showcase the scope of possibilities for displaying, arraying, and repurposing collectibles—be they museum-quality bibelots or garden-variety knickknacks. To demonstrate how to live with antiques and vintage objects in an elevated manner, no matter one's personal style and aesthetic preferences. To share inspiring examples of how collections can infuse and inform the surrounding decor—and how that decor can in turn act as a beautiful foil for those objects. And thus *Collected* was born.

We considered various ways to structure this book. Rather than focus on the collectibles themselves, we started thinking about the collectors. In our experience, collections are invariably an extension of their owner's personality, style, and quirks—a reflection of subliminal impulses and often irrational ardor. One fanatic goes bananas for all things fashion—from 1970s Gucci wallpaper to vintage Lilly Pulitzer and Goyard—while another loves the pop-art quality of overscale items. There are those who collect by palette or material. Some are pragmatists who collect useful objects (pitchers, scissors, galvanized buckets, stools), while others are seduced by out-and-out whimsy.

Many collecting styles are flip sides of the same coin: colorists love items in bold hues, neutralists favor muted tones. The exceptionalist thrills for rare examples of eighteenth-century Murano glass, the modest-ist covets everyday oddities like clothespins, penny jewelry, and homemade stuffed animals. The maximalist amasses a comprehensive compendium of their passion, while the minimalist is the most discerning of editors for whom three items says it all.

Parsing the differences between these methodologies became our organizing framework—and our obsession. We are fascinated by the innate instinct to gather and accumulate. So we grilled some of the most intriguing, stylish, and devoted collectors we knew to demystify what makes their approach unique, the motivation behind their pursuits, and how those twin influences guide their interior design sensibility. In so doing, we developed a sort of field guide to collectors. You will no doubt identify with one (or more) of the fifteen types—and gain insight into your own habits and tendencies. In fact, we deliberately omitted names of featured collectors, except for instances when a historic collection or a museum is highlighted, to make it easier to project yourself into the spaces illustrated, and to apply those ideas to your own home.

Common to all enthusiasts is a biological drive to treasure hunt coupled with a sense of discipline. Self-restraint is how collectors edit themselves and narrow their choices—a strategy they've devised to keep from being overwhelmed by the unfathomable bounty of the material world. The miniaturist focuses on small-scale objects; zoologists chase animal imagery; the fantasist ferrets out items that transport them on a great whimsy journey.

While the primary goal of assembling this book was to reveal the thoughtful beauty of and decorative principles behind various collections— from the accessible to the aspirational—we also wanted to celebrate the vast wonderment of the vintage world: the amazing handicrafts, materials, and objects at the flea-market junkie's disposal. Some seventy percent of collectors pursue tabletop items like china and pottery; we want to shine a spotlight on the enormous diversity of other (sometimes oddball) genres there are to collect. Pumpkin stems, amateur pet portraits, twine balls, Victorian tea tins, rug beaters. "Holy cow, I never even thought to collect that," you may find yourself saying. E-commerce has opened up the collecting market to a broader audience and made it easier to pursue such arcane items—whether you live in rural Idaho or blocks away from New York's antiques row.

We hope that an appreciation for all things old-school will encourage people to reconsider how they consume, and to go for a vintage piece when possible. Collecting is about recycling the wonderful things that already exist—without contributing to landfill. An added bonus, vintage goods are generally superior in conception and craft. A nineteenth-century ironstone platter often costs less than a new ceramic one and is infinitely more charming and durable. Steeping Earl Grey in a decades-old metal teapot creates a better brew.

In aspiring to showcase a wealth of vintage collectibles, our aim was breadth rather than depth: to feature as many subjects as possible. Accordingly, *Collected* is more sweeping survey than historical treatise. We are not trying to be encyclopedic, to showcase every kind of potholder or cookie cutter. Hopefully your curiosity will be piqued and you will be inspired to learn more about certain topics; there are whole books about many of these categories, from majolica to Native American basketweaving.

That said, readers will notice that many collectibles share a similar backstory, and these overarching narratives help contextualize objects. Decorative-arts history is very much informed by the availability or scarcity of certain resources, raw materials, and craft traditions. In the eighteenth and nineteenth centuries—the era that many featured items date from—makers were forced to use what was readily available to them. In many cases, that meant trash. Crafters in particular were extremely creative in repurposing discarded objects like spent matches, animal bones, fruit pits, and thrown-away packaging. The same maxim applied to commodities like indigo and cobalt, which were indigenous to specific cultures, and thus highly coveted by others (and accordingly exorbitant). The establishment of trade routes—between Europe and Asia, across the Mississippi River, etc.—abetted the conveyance of materials, skilled trades, and goods across the globe. Aesthetic traditions began "traveling" too, resulting in stylistic hybrids and cribbing of other cultures' artisanal traditions and sacred techniques.

Trafficking goods also meant tailoring them to the tastes of specific markets. Many items we value today as collectibles were initially conceived for the burgeoning tourist market, among them souvenir spoons and Grand Tour curios. Modern consumerism coincided with the rise of the middle class, rooted in the Industrial Revolution and the Victorian era. War times and the Great Depression—other periods marked by the admixture of scarcity, hyper-resourcefulness, and consumer desires—were hotbeds of invention and creativity, both by amateur crafters and large-scale makers who got increasingly savvy about branding and marketing.

Collected is not about celebrating who owns the biggest, rarest, or most expensive objects. Collecting is not inherently an elite pursuit. Rather, it is universal, accessible, and all-inclusive. Yes, there are those who chase obscure museum-caliber finds, but there's equal nobility and novelty in a collection of bottle caps salvaged from the recycling bin. You don't have to be a person of extraordinary means to be considered a collector. You just need to have a hunger for the pursuit, a thrill of the chase, and an openness to objects around you—and to welcoming joy into your life.

Outsider artist Robert Vasseur encrusted his home in Louviers, France, in a mindblowing mosaic of BROKEN CROCKERY. The project began as an impromptu wall embellishment in his kitchen and was extended to every surface of his house over the years. Vasseur worked on his mosaic from the 1950s until his death in 2002; now maintained by his son, the house is open for tours.

YOU DON'T NEED MONEY TO build a collection; doggedness and a sense of ingenuity are all that's required. The modest-ist embodies this credo, finding pleasure and whimsy in the hunting and handcrafting of throwaway items, often treating collectibles as fodder for DIY projects. A scrap-crafter at heart, the modest-ist makes vests from soda-can flip-tops, fashions bracelet charms from pennies, freehands stuffed animals from fabric scraps, and weaves candy wrappers into decorative boxes. The modest-ist aesthetic is humble, not show-offy: A collection of clothespins transformed into furniture cladding still retains a thrifty, humble vibe.

Coated-paper candy and cigarette-pack wrappers are popular collectibles for modest-ists, who fold and weave them into everything from purses to decorative objects. These WOVEN BOXES AND FRAMES are vintage examples, dating from around the 1930s. The collection is displayed on another genre of scrap craft: a table and shelf built from wooden spools.

These sorts of amateur craft projects were common during times when people repurposed as much household waste as possible. The Depression-era refrain of "waste not, want not" summarizes this motivation. Nineteenth- and early-twentieth-century modest-ists encrusted furniture in myriad odds and ends, such as canceled stamps, wooden spools, leather scraps, and food labels. Tin cans were clipped into dollhouse furniture or floral bouquets. Burnt matchsticks were another oft-used collectible salvaged from the trash; before the advent of electricity, households would light copious matches every day. Their ombré coloration can be found cladding boxes, furnishings, small accessories, and even miniature architectural replicas.

Over the years, amateur domestic handicrafts like rug hooking and cigar-box tramp art have become organized collecting markets. Folk art has gained a status on par with fine art, thanks to contemporary collectors' appreciation for all things quirky and handmade (i.e., the trained eye's appreciation of untrained talent). Spent bottle caps may have no value, but a vintage bottle-cap chain can fetch several hundred dollars.

These industrious hobbyists and scavengers are still active today. Instead of collecting burnt matchsticks they accumulate freebie matchbooks and cardboard pub coasters. Others salvage bottle caps or cigarette packaging. They see opportunity in the unwanted and take advantage of the amazing craft-supply store that is their own recycling bin. Their enthusiasms can veer a bit offbeat, such as used paper napkins, already-steeped tea bags, or depleted toothpaste tubes—curios that document and catalog daily consumption. But

everyday items like paper clips and skeins of twine are generally more their speed, the more mundane and cross-culturally ubiquitous the better.

What's important to the modest-ist is not just the particular subject they collect but also the opportunity it provides to amass a diverse variety. They are fascinated by the subtle nuances between similar objects. The modest-ist shares DNA with the maximalist, another collector motivated by abundance. That hyperacquisitive gene inspires the modest to display objects en masse, often in a humorously artsy manner. They might install a toilet-paper collection on a grid of TP holders in the loo, or cover the exterior of their home in a shimmery curtain of beer cans. The modest-ist also has a tendency to ball things up in an obsessive demonstration of plenitude—used tinfoil, smudged rubber bands from the daily newspaper delivery. (The legendary twelve-foot-tall ball of twine in Cawker City, Kansas? Textbook modest.)

While modest collectibles have become an elevated market, modest collecting remains a democratic, equal-opportunity style, courtesy of the low financial barrier to entry. (It's also something of a gateway drug to less modest collecting pursuits.) This is the most diverse category, since the modest-ist is anybody and everybody—from youngsters and artists to retirees. There's a little modest in all of us.

In the 1960s and 1970s, it was a common pastime to repurpose TIN CANS into whimsical furniture for dolls and dollhouses. They are easy to make, if somewhat laborious: Remove the lid, cut the sides into tiny strips, and then curlicue. Many of these vintage chairs were painted and given little upholstered seats, which were sometimes used as pincushions.

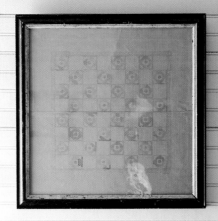

OPPOSITE The modest is often seduced by THREAD, STRING, AND YARN. Many save scraps and wind them into balls, but this collector seeks out full skeins of twine. A surprising diversity of shapes and styles exists, since every maker processes, wraps, and binds the twine a bit differently. He has gone to the far ends of the earth in pursuit of a global spectrum, buying BALLED TWINE from each country he visits.

THIS PAGE Old clothes and LEFTOVER SCRAPS from sewing projects are ideal for repurposing into stuffed animals—the cousin of the sock-monkey dynasty. Cute creatures are typically made from whatever's on hand—cotton, wool, terry cloth crochet, old socks—each fabric suggesting a different style of fur. While some hobbyists used patterns or copied the designs of commercially produced stuffed animals, most sewed freehand, using whatever size and shape of scraps were available. The ad hoc approach gives the animals the type of quirkiness and personality that collectors covet.

A unique spin on the prototypical coin collection: money jewelry. Vintage fanatics often encounter necklaces, earrings, pins, and bracelets made from pennies and sovereigns—whether homemade or commercially produced. Such adornments made smart use of essentially valueless coins, such as a handful of pesos or yuans amassed during travels.

OPPOSITE This collection includes a VICTORIAN MEDALLION BRACELET and one made from Mercury-head dimes. More exalted examples of the genre include the love token bracelet at top: One side of a coin was polished flat and monogrammed, and schoolgirls would trade them with friends to create charm bracelets. Below it is a bracelet fashioned from a pair of German silver dollars, sliced in half so the front and back imagery could be silhouetted separately.

THIS PAGE COPPER-PENNY JEWELRY is more modest, and almost always homemade. There are many techniques for crafting coins into personal adornments, from soldering them together to drilling holes that accommodate links. This collection also showcases bracelets made from Indian head pennies and buffalo nickels.

THIS PAGE This collector has been accruing a certain style of street art for more than fifteen years: PRIORITY MAIL STICKERS. He peels them off New York streetlights, signs, building facades, and other locations where the artists adhere them. He's intrigued by the talent demonstrated on these free canvases, and by the idea of being able to "own" graffiti, which is primarily a public art form. (Although free, the stickers don't come without a bit of effort: they are hard to peel intact.) The collection, which numbers more than 1,200, is stored on acid-free paper in archival boxes, grouped by year and style of postal sticker, which changed in format and design over the decades.

OPPOSITE Once a ubiquitous giveaway at restaurants and clubs, where they function as business cards, MATCHBOOKS have become less common as smoking in public areas falls out of favor. They are a fun and easy thing to collect, not only a sentimental keepsake of a trip or a great meal but also a survey of the history of graphic design and typography in miniature.

Finding himself with an abundance of free time, retired railway employee John Milkovisch began creating garlands of ALUMINUM BEER CANS and stringing them to the roof of his Houston home, like wind chimes. He started in 1968 and kept going until the entire clapboard house was covered, a feat that took an estimated fifty thousand cans.

Appropriately named the Beer Can House, the property is a marriage of practicality and absurdity, recycling and refinement. The shimmery METAL CLADDING was both decorative and functional, helping lower energy bills. While many tout the creation as folk art (the house is now a museum, open to the public), Milkovisch considered his hobby to be pure amusement.

THIS PAGE The modest version of philately: collecting stamps to repurpose as decoration. STAMPCRAFT was a practical diversion during an era when mail was the primary medium for interpersonal communication, and delivered multiple times a day. A Victorian-era étagère is decoupaged in whole stamps, applied in mosaic fashion. Displayed upon it is a collection of milk glass plates embellished with imagery snipped from postage.

OPPOSITE Stamp crafters would cut out fields of color or whole motifs like faces to create PICTORIAL COLLAGES, such as this basket of flowers.

William B Pike

THIS PAGE A U.K.-based artist has amassed more than thirty thousand used TEA BAGS, all from pots of brew she's consumed by herself or with friends. They form the basis of a recent series of artworks: She dries the bags on paper to document the stains they leave behind—a sort of diaristic documentation of her life. The dried bags, stored in suitcases in her studio, are equally beautiful and intriguing.

OPPOSITE The humble CLOTHESPIN comes in myriad shapes, scales, materials, and functions. In addition to the garden-variety style used to hang wet garments on clotheslines, there are ones used for desktop organizers (often large and either Lucite or brass) and for drying photographs in a darkroom. This gathering is a trail of invention and ingenuity—some are crazy Rube Golberg-esque contraptions.

FOLLOWING SPREAD Bottle caps are one part trash, one part "pop" art (pardon the pun). Often collected in their own right, the metal disks are also a favorite fodder of folk artists, the fixation of an entire craft category. Akin to matchbooks, a collection of BOTTLE CAPS is a veritable timeline of beverage fads and themes.

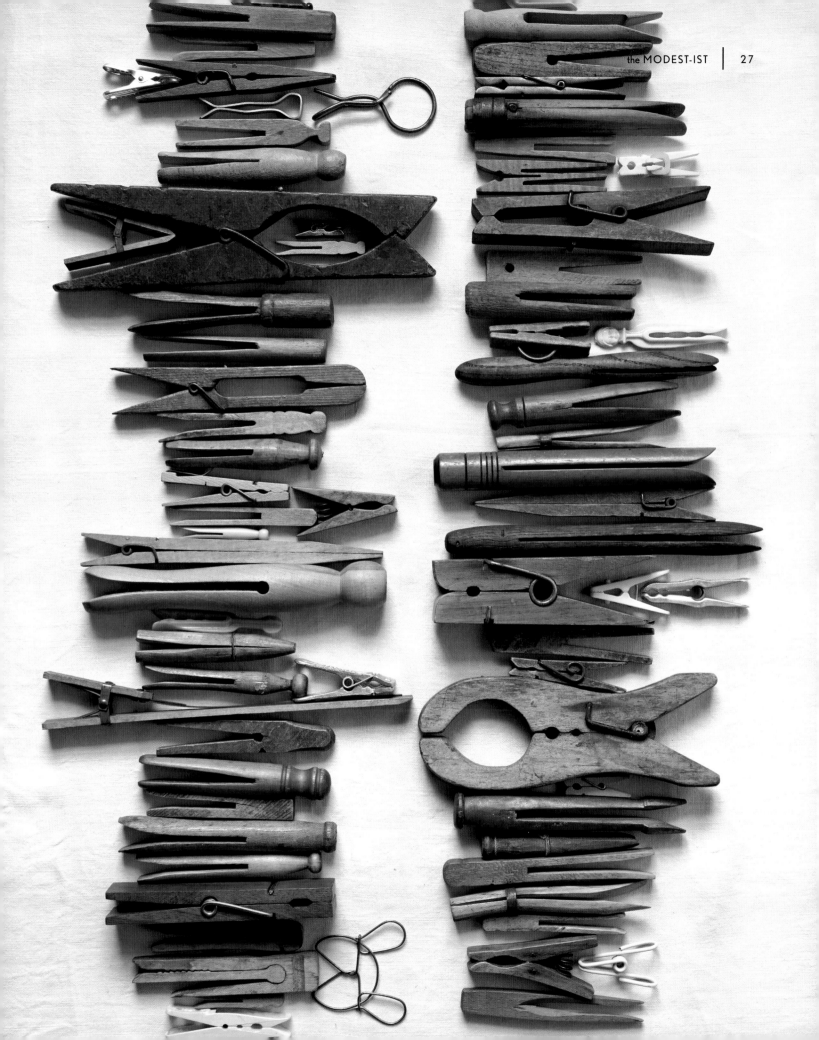

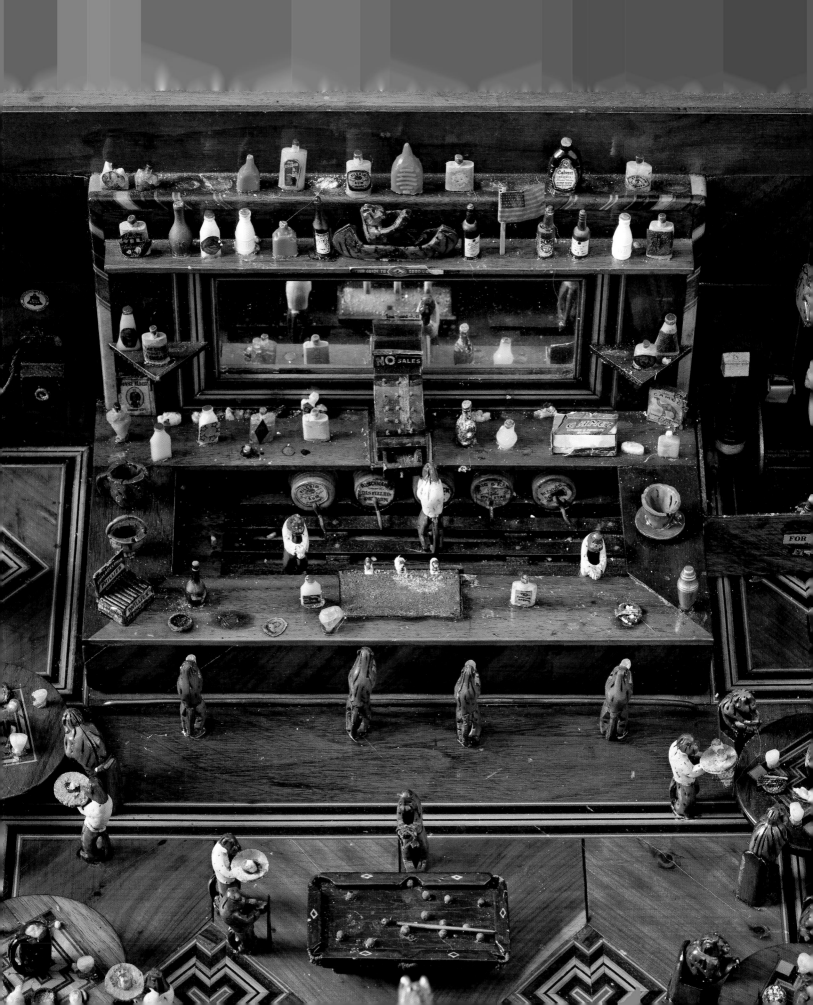

OPPOSITE Many SCRAP CRAFTS were executed by amateur artisans whiling away extreme downtime: riding out a cold winter, amusing themselves during a long boat trip, or serving time in captivity. Prisoners were by necessity resourceful, using various kitchen scraps to create elaborate straw marquetry, gaming pieces, and bottle art. Some envisioned whole fantasy worlds, such as this saloon scene with woodwork fashioned from cigar boxes, liquor bottles made from old toothbrush handles, and monkeys chiseled from peach pits.

THIS PAGE Peach pits were a popular medium for crafters, who carved them into little sculptures. Vintage hunters will discover an incredible variety of motifs—chamber pots, canoes, soup tureens, rabbits, tiny furnishings—but the most common subjects were baskets and little monkeys. Here a gathering of PEACH-PIT SIMIANS relaxes in a miniature pool hall.

These miniscule BASKETS, all carved from fruit pits and nut shells, are the handiwork of a single amateur craftsman. Arrayed on a funky homemade rack, the baskets each have their own little personality. This pit crafter was a purist, creating the baskets out of a single nut shell, whereas other hobbyists cobbled them together from different pieces.

Some CARVED FRUIT PITS could be elaborate in execution, but these rough-hewn baskets and figurines are quite rudimentary in style. In addition to peach pits, crafters would sometimes use nectarines or cherry pits. Projects like this don't necessarily demand advanced artistry and skill; tenacity and creativity are most important.

THE EXCEPTIONALIST seeks out only the best and most unique. If the object isn't rarified, they're not interested. But for this collector, value isn't about provenance or even price. While the items they covet—cameo shells, majolica furniture, nineteenth-century engraved glassware—may be super luxurious (and often super expensive), the exceptionalist is not interested in collecting as an investment or an exercise in commodity trading. The exceptionalist's trove reflects the best-executed workmanship, the most talented artisan, the most precious material, the most complicated technologies, the most intense craftsmanship—examples of extreme beauty, extreme skill, and extreme quality.

This nineteenth-century tumbler epitomizes the superhuman skill the exceptionalist covets: Miniature scenes or elaborate patterns rendered with chiaroscuro shading are WATER-ENGRAVED into paper-thin glass—a technique mastered by English, Irish, and Bohemian craftsmen.

The exceptionalist is typically highly focused. Their collections are often mind-bogglingly, even absurdly specific—a genre within a genre. They collect not "micromosaics" but micromosaic architectural scenes; not "silhouettes" but full-figured silhouettes of people posed alongside furniture. This specificity derives from two impulses. On one hand, it makes the pursuit all the more thrilling. On the other, it's a form of discipline and restraint. Exceptionalists are so bowled over by the rich bounty of the material world and the decorative arts that they have to limit themselves by concentrating on an obscure subset—and set themselves up for a more challenging hunt. Self-limiting is a defense against dilettantism (not to mention bankruptcy and hoarding). They are the severest of editors, taking exception to anything too ordinary, pedestrian, or easily found or created.

The exceptionalist understands that collecting is not just a fun pastime but a huge responsibility. They consider themselves custodians. Possessions such as rare Venetian marbled glass demand that their owners have the psychological and financial means to take on the task of caring for them. This is a collecting style that rewards intensity and tenacity: The exceptionalist may find only one or two pieces a year that meet all their criteria, and will go to any ends in pursuit of them.

A common theme of exceptionalist collections is the demonstration of the international trade of skill and materials. Many of the craft traditions they pursue are localized to a particular time and place, be it sixteenth-century China or eighteenth-century Italy. The objects tell the story of modern globalization: The tailoring of goods to the tastes of different markets, cross-cultural influences and interpretations, the emigration of European artisans, and the flow of foreign goods to the emergent middle-class American consumer in the Victorian period.

While the exceptionalist is not preoccupied by provenance per se, the context and audience for which their collectibles were initially made is an appealing part of the story and a factor in their interest. The consumers who formerly owned these possessions had an increasingly global outlook as well, especially as travel became more feasible and accessible. Epitomizing that concept is the Grand Tour phenomenon, a rite of passage for upper-class Europeans and Americans, as well as other persons of learning in the seventeenth and eighteenth centuries. Heeding the lure of the foreign and exotic—and the promise of cultural cred—these tourists visited all the classical wonders, purchasing portable keepsakes (lava souvenirs, marble obelisks) along the way.

While many exceptionalists own museum-quality pieces, they do not hide them away under lock and key. Exceptionalists prefer to live among their passions, like embedded reporters. Their homes inevitably reflect their collecting sensibility: their furnishings and finish choices bespeak a purity and quality of material. Tableau are rearranged and pieces moved around often so they can be seen afresh and in new contexts; juxtapositions are conceived to spark a lively, polyglot dialogue. There is much to learn from the exceptionalist's embrace of tablescaping, their sophisticated color sense, their unpretentious approach to precious things, and their belief in the quality of their surroundings—and the importance of the personal environment—above all else. Their collections may at first glance seem a bit serious, but if you look closely you see the whimsy, eccentricity, and infectious joy that they convey.

Micromosaics are fashioned from tiny slivers of glass painstakingly arrayed to create pint-sized pictorial masterpieces. The technique was often used to embellish jewelry, decorative boxes, and even furnishings like tabletops. This collector has a very focused interest: MICROMOSAIC depictions of architecture, from classical follies to ancient ruins. Such pieces were generally made as Grand Tour souvenirs, their small size ensuring affordability and easy transport.

THIS PAGE Some of the best examples of jewelry-like CAMEO SHELLS are from Torre del Greco, Italy, a coastal town that became a center of the cameo trade in the eighteenth century. Artisans would select the very best shells—unbroken, perfectly weathered, beautifully shaped—and hand carve the intricate designs, which ranged from silhouetted visages to Greek myths. The most detailed could take a craftsman weeks to execute.

OPPOSITE Some collectors focus laser-like on a particular item or material category; others obsess over a specific place and/or time. This exceptionalist is emphatically the latter, specializing in SCANDINAVIAN FURNISHINGS. Throughout the house, one geographic area is seen through the centuries and varied design movements—from Edwardian accessories and a Gustavian settee to 1930s art deco lighting.

THE CHALKY TEXTURE
OF THE WALL PAINT
BALANCES WITH THE SOFT
PATINA OF THE METAL
AND GILT DETAILS.

THE PINK-ORANGE WALL PAINT
PROVIDES A RADIANT FOIL FOR
THE OTHERWISE CALM, NEUTRAL
TONES OF THE FURNITURE AND
ACCESSORIES, WHICH GET THEIR
COLORATION FROM NATURAL
MATERIALS.

OPPOSITE Antique snuffboxes are treated as jewelry for the home, accenting various surfaces. The homeowner's decor mimics the mood of his collection, featuring a diversity of rich materials and GLOBAL ORIGINS: Vesuvius-themed artworks from Italy, a Russian sofa, a French marble-top side table, a Swedish painted-wood side chair, a Baltic crystal girandole, and, below the Italian table, a German silver tazza.

THIS PAGE Designed to house powdered tobacco, SNUFF-BOXES were like today's high-end watch: a functional object that was also a personal accessory—and thus a signifier of social status and taste. This connoisseur's collection, dating from the seventeenth to nineteenth centuries, showcases varied techniques and an array of precious materials, including mastodon horn, ivory, pudding stone, and even British coins. Displaying disparate designs together celebrates their variety.

The establishment of trade routes between Asia and the West sparked a craving for Chinese decorative objects, from lacquerware to fine porcelain. These handicrafts inspired not only covetousness but also copycats. Despite European artisans' efforts to mimic the graceful hand painting of Chinese export porcelain, the beauty of the real thing remains unparalleled—which is at the root of its desirability, both then and now.

CUSTOMIZE SIMPLE SHELVES FOR DISPLAY VIA PLATE STANDS AND PEDESTALS, PAINTED THE SAME COLOR AS THE WALL BEHIND SO THEY RECEDE FROM VIEW.

The Chinese were the first—and, until the eighteenth century, only—artisans to produce PORCELAIN DISHWARE. Viewed up close, it seems inconceivable that such precise patterning was executed by hand, so flawless and machine-like is the brushwork. Chinese porcelain came in many HUES AND MOTIFS, reflecting the localized tastes of the many markets it was exported to. Modern-day devotees can take advantage of this chromatic diversity, collecting pieces that share a colorway, if not a design, for a cohesive look.

The Venetian island of Murano, Italy, is famous for its glassblowing studios, which took root in the late 1200s. Of the many styles produced there over the centuries, CALCEDONIO is perhaps the rarest. The name derives from the Latin word for chalcedony, whose striated, marbled appearance the glasswork mimics. Rendered in rich but earthen hues, the semi-opaque glass was originally produced by a single factory for a brief run. Despite the extremely limited production, the medium was a hotbed of formal inventiveness. To wit: These vessel designs range from proto-modernist profiles to riffs on ancient classical forms and Chinese Ming pottery.

It takes a tenacious personality to collect this obscure, elusive glassware, which makes the existence of this particular compilation all the more amazing. Originally amassed by one collector, the vessels were later auctioned off and then purchased en masse by a single dealer. In an attempt to reassemble the collection, the current owner has been purchasing pieces one by one as they're released back onto the market. He is driven by his love of the objects themselves as well as by a sense of responsibility for keeping the collection intact. Hence his decision to display them together, like an extended family.

The venerable tradition of SILHOUETTE PORTRAITURE, which crescendoed in the late eighteenth and early nineteenth centuries, encompasses a variety of media, from hand-cut paper to ink drawings. Typical of the exceptionalist, this collector narrowed his enthusiasm to an extreme: He buys only positive-image full-figure silhouettes (profiles from the neck up are most common), depicted with furniture. Matching gold-leaf frames unify the collection.

This 1828 work is by famed French silhouettist AUGUSTE EDOUART, who was prolific and well traveled—not to mention insanely talented. In the early nineteenth century, Edouart toured England and the Eastern seaboard as a featured attraction at society bashes, where he'd create a likeness of each guest, bestowed as a party favor. The artist drew and cut his works freehand, making two copies of each—one for his subject, one for his own archives.

Porcelain salvaged from shipwrecks is extremely collectible, given the difficulty of retrieving undersea cargo—not to mention its swashbuckling backstory. It is quite literally sunken treasure, with all the exoticism and intrigue that the phrase implies. (Luckily, porcelain withstands salt water quite well.) Valuables rescued by marine archeologists centuries after sinking are generally sold via auction, and the majority wind up in museums. These troves made it into private hands.

THIS PAGE These salvaged blue-and-white CHINESE VASES were given a second lease on life in this museum-like Paris home, placed on wall-mounted pedestals that extend to the ceiling in diamond-shape configurations.

OPPOSITE This tastemaker embraced the challenge of displaying a profusion of repetitive multiples—all the same scale and pattern—by playing up the sameness. Setting the vases on a rococo GILT-WORK MIRROR conjures a look of drama and abundance, the reflective surface creating the illusion of an infinite amount.

You know you're an exceptionalist when you have bronze statues and OLD MASTERS DRAWINGS ... in your closet. For the enjoyment of yourself alone. (The fact that they're all nudes adds cheeky humor.) This ultra-chic lair was the dressing area of fashion icon Bill Blass's New York apartment. Even his suits and shoes were arranged as a precious collection, hung from a gilded pole and spaced just so.

Parisian label Goyard was a favorite of the French aristocracy in the nineteenth century; cultural figures such as Coco Chanel, Edith Piaf, and Pablo Picasso in the twentieth; and fashionistas of all stripes today. This fanatic has been amassing VINTAGE TRUNKS AND BAGS for more than twenty-five years and has embraced the hallowed tradition of getting his monogram hand-painted in the company's trademark style, complete with racing stripe and correct placement of the lettering. Trunks can be a practical item to collect: Use them to store possessions, stack a trio to create a side table, or corral a shapely grouping for an effect verging on pop art.

The same maximalist has a nose for PERFUME BOTTLES, too, as evidenced by his rather copious horde. He is a coveter of all things fashion—even the wallpaper is Gucci.

In the seventeenth century, water engraving was executed by a craftsman operating a cutting wheel—a rather aggressive piece of machinery for such a delicate canvas. It took an insane amount of talent to control the wheel, to know just how much pressure to apply and which angle created what type of cut, and to not make a single mistake on an entire piece of superthin glass.

A cut-glass HURRICANE dances candlelight and patterned shadows around a room, an effect intensified by the age-old trick of placing a mirror behind the light source. The crispness of the engraving contrasts beautifully with the mottled patina of the antique mirror glass.

This magical pictorial tumbler, a seventeenth-century WEDDING GLASS, depicts a dessert service set on a lace tabletop. The object was so precious to its owner that it was repaired on one side with a staple, a bygone practice for suturing broken glass and china.

Unlike some of the local-
ized artisanal handicrafts
showcased in this chapter,
MAJOLICA was a
relatively global and
mass-market phenomenon.
During the Victorian era,
when the centuries-old art
form experienced a revival,
the colorful tin-glazed
earthenware was made by
dozens of studios in numerous countries—Italy, France,
Germany, England,
America, Spain, Portugal,
etc. What's so intriguing
about majolica isn't the skill
behind it—although there
exist superior examples of
glazing and molding—so
much as the whimsical
conception.

Elevate graphic MAJOLICA PLATTERS to the status of fine artwork by hanging them salon-style. A neutral but textured backdrop—such as this grasscloth wall covering—forms a rich but sedate anchor for the colorful glazing and exuberant motifs, a fun mix of mossy, boggy plants. The tables below are majolica, too, designed with Victorian domestic conservatories in mind.

Sheffield plate is fabricated of thin silver sheets fused to copper, a technique developed in the mid-eighteenth century to mimic solid sterling. Prior to then, only the aristocracy and the clergy could afford sterling objects; Sheffield plate made fine metalwork accessible to an upper-middle class audience. Its heyday was short-lived: The invention of electroplating in 1840 rendered Sheffield plate obsolete, ensuring its future status as a collector's item.

Enthusiasts value SHEFFIELD PLATE'S beautiful luster. Unlike electroplated metal, which has a hard shine, Sheffield plate took on a soft velvety quality. With use, the outer layer of sterling would wear down so the underlying copper shone through—a quality valued by contemporary collectors but not by nineteenth-century homeowners, who typically had it replated. Pieces that have not been refurbished garner top price today.

Sheffield plate was used to make all manner of household tools, such as GRAPE SCISSORS AND WICK SNUFFERS—items that, like the material they're made of, are obsolete today.

THE USUAL DEFINITION of a collector is someone who amasses multiples of a certain thing. The minimalist is the exception to this rule, living among a judicious few prized possessions. It is not unusual to find in the minimalist's museum-like lair one chair, one table, one bed, one piece of art, and one accessory. They are the severest of curators, with an unparalleled degree of restraint. For every piece they buy, they'll turn down twenty that are almost, but not quite, right. Diana Vreeland's famous quip sums up their collecting philosophy: Elegance is refusal.

Minimalists mine every opportunity to create canny juxtapositions. In a snug vestibule, an artwork by Mike and Doug Starn echoes the constructivist form of a 1930s FRENCH CHAIR. Leather wall cladding enhances the subtle play of textures.

The minimalist ethos is about fewer—but better. Or, rather, *their favorite*. These collectors have a fantastic eye and incredibly exacting standards. They are seduced only by superior examples of their passions: the most obscure Thonet chair prototype, an artfully patinated eighteenth-century mirror with silvering peeling just so. Whereas most of us make compromises in our abodes—tolerating a too-small couch while in search of the perfect one—this collector would rather go without than own anything subpar. The minimalist mindset: Why live with something you don't absolutely *love*?

That said, there is a quality of endless striving to the minimalist, a sort of perpetual editor who's constantly reevaluating, upgrading, and honing their possessions. Indulging their perfectionist streak, they thrill to trading up, and as a result their home is in constant flux. Most collectors wouldn't dream of parting with one of their mid-century Italian glass decanters or vintage Vera scarves just because they bought another; abundance is part of the fun. For this collector, however, one thing in means one thing out. Scoring a 1960s wire sculpture at an antiques shop necessitates downsizing the C. Jeré wall hanging.

The minimalist is all about discipline—not only mental but also visual. They crave clarity and order, resulting in a home that's spare to the point of being reductive. It's not that the minimalist doesn't have worldly possessions; they just can't *live* with lots of things cluttering up sight lines. Books, extra sets of dishware, family photos—these are typically compartmentalized elsewhere, kept in a weekend home or stashed in oversized closets. Or in their offices: The minimalist is commonly a fashion designer, architect, dealer, artist, or other such aesthete who's immersed in visual stimulation all day long and demands an antidote to that at home.

In such a pared-down environment, each object invites contemplation— much more so than in other collecting scenarios, which tend to be about the sum of the parts. Every piece in the minimalist's home becomes pregnant with meaning, and the relationship between them likewise imperative. While many people display their various collections together (commingling vintage snuffboxes with marble busts, for instance) to create a lively frisson, like the background murmur at a cocktail party, the minimalist's home is so austere that the dialogue between each piece is fully engaged and fully audible.

For the minimalist, the environment in which the collection lives is of equal importance to the collection itself. They favor white walls and white or black floors, which silhouette furnishings like sculptures. Stripped-down architecture and sedate but über-luxurious finishes reinforce the vibe of airiness and calm. Indeed, you'd be forgiven for thinking that the minimalist is collecting plain air. Their less-is-more approach extends to the building envelope: Why have a span of eight windows when you could have just one giant sheet of glass? Why have multiple paint colors when one— decorator's white—will reflect every color under the sun depending on the light conditions? The minimalist prioritizes quality of space over quantity of consuming.

FOLLOWING SPREAD Quality trumps quantity in the minimalist's aerie. White walls, ebonized floors, and deadpan architectural details make the precious few furnishings stand out like sculptures. Austerity need not preclude luxury: Note the obsidian BEDSPREAD in sumptuous Mongolian lamb.

THIS PAGE Minimalism infuses every corner of this abode. Even the portraiture is reductive: SILHOUETTES of the homeowners. The art form pares down representation to its most reductive essence, i.e., just a simple gestural outline of the facial features.

OPPOSITE Another object invites contemplation and comparison in the gallery-esque setting: The agitated line of a mid-century WIRE SCULPTURE—like a scribble drawn in thin air. The homeowner adhered to a minimalist color palette throughout: just black, white, and a touch of green.

© MOLE & THOMAS
915 MEDINAH BLDG.
CHICAGO, ILL.

HUMAN STATUE OF LIBERTY
18,000 OFFICERS AND MEN
AT
CAMP DODGE, DES MOINES IA.
COL. WM. NEWMAN, COMMANDING
COL. RUSH S. WELLS, DIRECTING.

THE MAXIMALIST THINKS BIG. They collect multiples of a certain object, and the sheer volume of their holdings astounds; tallies in the tens of thousands are not unusual. This personality type is the polar opposite of the exceptionalist, who chases only obscure items of limited availability. The maximalist, in contrast, pursues a topic with no end, a genre defined by infinite quantity and variety: postcards, takeout menus, neckties, mirrors, dice. Such collections inevitably beg the question "Just how long have you been collecting?" It is an incredible achievement to amass 1,500 printed cloth napkins, to practically document the history of a consumer category; the maximalist is nothing if not ambitious. In addition to large quantities, they also love large

---

The "LIVING PORTRAITS" of early-twentieth-century photographers Arthur Mole and John Thomas exemplify the maximalist's interest in collectibles that themselves suggest multiplicity. The duo's famous depiction of the Statue of Liberty is actually an assemblage of eighteen thousand soldiers at Camp Dodge in Des Moines, Iowa. Inspecting the photographs up close, you can discern the individual soldiers; a label at the bottom of each photo tells how many men it took to make it.

things, like overscaled furniture, giant funnels, and jumbo-size liquor-bottle factices originally used as bar and store displays. If they can get their hands on the largest, even better: the most gargantuan ironstone cake stand, the biggest blown-glass dome. More is definitely more.

Although plenitude is the goal, the maximalist is not undiscriminating. Like other collectors, maximalists follow rules that they establish to limit themselves, be it a price cap or a particular color palette, or devotion to a certain designer or manufacturer. Condition is still important. In categories such as toys, neckties, and books, it's common practice for collectors to buy the same exact thing over and over, each time trading up until they get a superior example—although not everything in their collection needs to be pristine, since the whole supersedes the parts.

The object of the maximalist's affection may start out broad, and narrow over time: from playing cards in general to nineteenth-century travel decks. Or they begin subcategorizing, curating various collections within their collection. After years spent amassing an exhaustive compendium of pot holders, they begin pursuing red-and-white homemade, crocheted pot holders in the shape of pants. The maximalist knows that such specificity is absurd, but it's how they keep life interesting. (It's also an acknowledgment that humor is part of the package.)

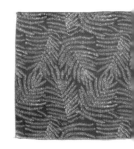

The opposite scenario is just as likely to occur: A collection that started off quite modest in scope or focused in topic expands (sometimes spontaneously) to become more all-encompassing—evolving from a grouping of mid-century Scandinavian decanters to a massive assemblage of

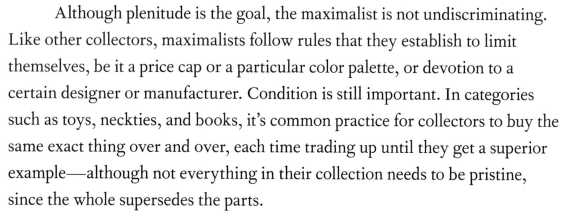

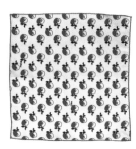

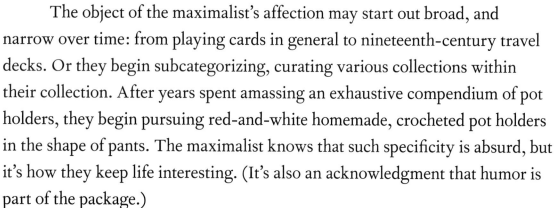

the MAXIMALIST | 71

vintage glassware of all stripes. They'll tell themselves, "Oh, just one more beautiful piece of white ironstone"—and suddenly it's spiraled into madness. Maximalists are the bowerbirds of the collecting world, constantly bringing home new pieces, sometimes by the carload. This phenomenon is simply a consequence of the maximalist's acquisitive impulse. All collectors derive satisfaction and a sense of achievement from scoring a great find, but the maximalist needs that fix more regularly. (Which is often why they seek out such commonplace items: The success rate is high.)

Hundreds of plateau mirrors, a library of graphic-design history books—when you live with so many of a certain thing, organization and display are inevitably challenging. Especially since the maximalist likes to showcase, not store, their stuff. What would be the point of owning five hundred Thermoses if they're all kept in boxes in the basement, rarely to see the light of day? The prevalent strategy is containment, corralling goods into cabinets, display cases, shelves, or other frameworks that draw a physical boundary around the collection to keep it in check. Another option is to embrace artful explosion, allowing the collection to create its own framework: books stacked in sculptural piles on the floor, white crockery overtaking every wall of the kitchen like a site-specific art installation.

The maximalist approaches their hobby with largesse. One maximalist in this chapter collects crystal vases, thrift-store books, South American silver, perfume bottles, and Peruvian voodoo objects—and that's just a start. For the maximalist, it's all about the sum of the parts.

Mid-century artist Vera Neumann became a textile phenomenon in the 1950s, designing everything from housewares to sportswear bedecked in her signature sunny prints. Among her devoted fan base is this maximalist, who collects VERA NAPKINS—but just one of every pattern. The prints are quite varied, as Neumann was fluent in both abstraction and figuration, and in various media, from watercolor to paper collage. Courtesy of their small size and square format, the napkins themselves look like little canvases.

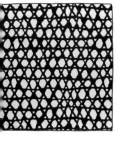

While antique mirrors entice enthusiasts of all stripes, they are particularly apropos for the maximalist, visually doubling their other collections. The genre offers many subcategories to specialize in: compacts, mirror plateaus, handheld and convex mirrors, et cetera. Until the mid-nineteenth century, when silver-coating was developed, looking glasses were made from polished sheet metal fused to a thick piece of cut glass.

THIS PAGE Mirror plateaus were a fixture of nineteenth-century dining rooms. Placed in the center of the table and set with candles, these reflective surfaces were a clever source of uplighting; they were also used atop dressers and vanities to corral perfume and small bottles. (Most are backed with felt or little feet, and some companies made dual-use designs that could hang as well.) Up close, you can revel in the custom ending CUTWORK AND ENGRAVING as well as the beautifully mottled patina of the antique glass. This collector aspired to amass as many shapes and patterns as possible, gravitating to clean geometric designs.

OPPOSITE This maximalist lined his bathroom in superior examples of the genre, arranging them on THIN LEDGES made from simple stock moldings.

THE BUTTERY YELLOW
PAINT COLOR PLAYS
BEAUTIFULLY OFF THE
SILVER TONES OF THE
AGED, NICKEL-FRAME
MIRRORS.

Crockery and WHITE IRONSTONE are perennially popular collecting categories. This is a particularly advanced example of both obsessions: The collection overtakes the entire kitchen, casually stored in an allover installation that fully fills a hutch and the surrounding wall space—yet there's always room to squeeze in just one more.

An architect outfitted the bathroom of his 1800s Sag Harbor, New York, cottage in a salon-like installation of **DARK-FRAMED MIRRORS**, mostly flea-market finds. There's something playfully absurd about showcasing so grand and abundant a collection in such a small, private space. But it makes good sense: A multiplicity of mirrors helps amplify light and create views in window-challenged rooms while offering the impression of more loftlike surroundings.

A pop-modernist artist gravitates to collectibles with a similarly cheeky sensibility and offbeat sense of scale. To wit: Among the many oddball things he collects are GIANT LIQUOR BOTTLES— some nearly four feet tall—called factices that were originally used as pub and shop displays.

Appropriately, the maximalist arranged the pieces in a faux-bar setup in a dining room, where they spill over from a storage unit to adjacent floor space. In a domestic context, the pieces' outsize proportions look especially witty.

More than five hundred metal-bodied vintage THERMOS BOTTLES—the byproduct of a twenty-five-year collecting effort—fill this maximalist's loft. Lined up in militant rows on a series of built-in shelves, the colorful vacuum flasks become a decorative element that celebrates plenitude. The installation also nods to a bygone era when seemingly every student and office worker toted around a thermos of hot soup.

THE HUMAN LIBERTY BELL
25000 OFFICERS & MEN
AT
CAMP DIX, NEW JERSEY
GENERAL HUGH L. SCOTT, COM'DR.

Arthur Mole and John Thomas shot their photos from air-raid towers, using an eleven-by-fourteen view camera. Thomas directed his subjects with a megaphone; Mole clicked the shutter. These incredible performance-art pieces were conceived to promote war bonds during World War I, and the imagery is appropriately patriotic: an eagle, Uncle Sam, military insignias, Woodrow Wilson's profile, flags, et cetera.

THIS PAGE To create this likeness of the LIBERTY BELL (complete with signature crack), the artists painstakingly arranged 25,000 soldiers—some wearing white, others wearing black—on a field at New Jersey's Camp Dix.

OPPOSITE The PRINTS were sold in a number of formats—from small postcards to large (and rare) sixteen-by-twenty glossies—and were often reprinted in newspapers on Veterans Day. Readers would clip and frame them, which is often what you'll find in vintage shops.

THE LIVING UNCLE SAM

No. of officers and men, 19,000. Taken at Camp Lee, Petersburg, Va. Major General Omar Bundy Com'd'r. Ground measurements: width of hat rim, 132 ft.; height of hat, 415 ft.; width of top of hat, 526 ft.; width of bottom of picture, 45 ft.; total length, 605 ft. No. of men in head and shoulders, 3,400; No. of men in hat, 15,600. Copyright 1919. Mole & Thomas 915 Medinah Bldg., Chicago, Ill. Original Photograph, 11 x 14 — $1.00.

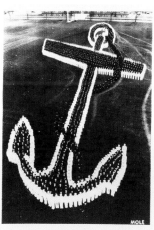

2200 Recruits Under Training at U. S. NAVAL TRAINING STATION, GREAT LAKES, ILLINOIS REAR ADMIRAL, JOHN DOWNES U S NAVY, COMMANDING OFFICER

PREVIOUS SPREAD A thrift-store fanatic has amassed thousands of NECKTIES over the years, four hundred of which are from the same maker: Rooster. The Philadelphia brand, which operated from the 1950s through 1980s, was famous for its flat-bottomed style and charming imagery of various professions (dentist, aviator pilot, bridge engineer). These early examples were block printed on heavy cotton in four colors, giving them a Warhol feel.

THIS PAGE The Rooster enthusiast stashes most of his collection on a tie tree in his bedroom, so overstuffed that it looks like a colorful Cousin It. VINTAGE TIES are hard to find in pristine shape— they're inevitably marred with food stains, neck grease, and cigarette burns—which only stokes the maximalist's lust, inviting them to trade up until they find their favorite pattern in their preferred color— and in mint condition.

OPPOSITE This maximalist collects vintage PATTERNED PANTS, primarily cotton. The majority are American made and date from the 1960s through 1990s, with an emphasis on the swinging seventies. His favorites, showcased in a Lucite trunk at the foot of a guest bed, are but a fraction of the collection, which ranges from country club attire to casual sportswear.

WHAT IS DRAGGING ME?

I am unhappy because I am not perfect. If I want to be better than everyone else & I want to be unique and I do not know that I am unique! I want to be unique by being better — this is a false premise. This feeling keeps me in a state of tension which I seem to enjoy. As long as I enjoy this tension I cannot be creative. Use the tension instead of enjoying it. Go through the pain rather than sitting on it for truly creative productivity.

I have to make a greater effort to take better care of myself beginning with my body and my eating habits.

*I don't like where I'm at now (but do not perfect) and instead I want to be there (god state) now & I don't want to work for this because I know deep down inside that I never can be god-like, so, though, I don't give up, I never work really for what I can do — namely MY BEST. And this way I get into the comparing state which is Death because as soon as I start to compare myself & I loose my uniqueness. I can only do mine and what is in me and the more I know myself, this self will then come out in my work.

BERND UND HILLA BECHER

KÖLNISCHER KUNSTVEREIN

There are card collectors who set their sights on just one suit or face card, like hearts or aces, queens or jacks, and then there's the 52 Plus Joker Club that pursues complete vintage decks. Can you guess what maximalists go after? Full sets, of course—and the more the merrier. Cards are a collecting category with myriad subgenres: handmade decks, assorted shapes, smaller-sized children's and travel sets, and transformation decks, embellished with drawings that incorporate the pips.

OPPOSITE A collection of PLAYING CARDS can present an organizational challenge. Why not show off their graphic forms by utilizing them as embellishment, as with this clever do-it-yourself decoupaged folding screen?

THIS PAGE Playing cards come in an array of tantalizing formats: round, crooked, ovoid, and more. The patterns are amazingly diverse, too, from pictorial motifs to repetitive fields of pattern. This collector seeks out myriad styles, but all in a SINGLE COLORWAY. When the cards are not out on display, he stores them in vintage cases designed to look like little leather-bound books.

POT HOLDERS are an open-ended collecting genre, so commonplace are these kitchen staples. This collection offers a peek into the maximalist mindset: As it grew more abundant (despite a self-imposed three-dollar price limit), the collector started to pursue ever more rarefied subgenres. First, he narrowed his enthusiasm to homemade versions only, and then crocheted (versus patchwork) designs. Next he limited the palette to red and white, and the subject to just pants and shorts.

THIS PAGE Exaggerated scale is a lure for this maximalist; note the supersized folding ruler. He also collects a specific shape: FACETED GEOMETRIC FORMS, rendered in wood, plastic, metal, glass, and pottery.

OPPOSITE Pressed-glass plates have whimsical shapes and decorative, frilly edges. The high-water mark of the genre was the Victorian era, when the molding technique was perfected, resulting in elaborate designs. This enthusiast collects CLEAR GLASS only, hung in a tight cluster on one wall. The absence of color—save for a single plate tinted the palest green—keeps the vignette from looking too busy and allows the maximalist to hang multiples. Installed across from a window, they cast striking shadows on the wall behind, allowing enhanced appreciation of the plates' lovely (but hard-to-see) detailing.

OPPOSITE A hallway lined with floor-to-ceiling shelving provides an organizing framework for a maximalist's collection of books on the history of graphic design. He devotes an entire shelf to mid-century designer Alvin Lustig, another to art director Paul Rand. In addition to MONOGRAPHS on their work, he also collects book jackets and other objects that these talents designed.

THIS PAGE On the opposite end of the spectrum, this bibliophile stores his tomes in PLENTIFUL PILES on the floor beside his bed, where they double as nightstands. The rest of his voluminous collection is stashed on bookshelves; these are just recent thrift-store acquisitions he's currently enjoying— the circulating shelves versus the library stacks, if you will.

Vintage bandannas have become a major obsession of late, with fashion brands from J. Crew to Ralph Lauren reproducing period designs. Crafty salvagers can often score these pert patterned squares for next to nothing at swap meets and flea markets, and use them for all sorts of do-it-yourself creations.

Framed bandannas hung in a tight grid celebrate the plenitude of graphic patterns and border styles. Below is a stylish dog bed sewn from a pair of bandannas.

An inexpensive hollow-core door from Home Depot gets a high-style makeover when decorated with a patchwork of OLD-SCHOOL BANDANNAS. A trestle base and protective top surface of vinyl laminate—edged with nail heads tracing the fabric print—renders it a serviceable work surface. Bandannas were also adhered to the trash can via wallpaper paste, creating a coordinating desk set.

This collector has acquired SNUFFBOXES of varied styles, eras, and materials—some elaborate, others more workaday. Among the diverse subgenres he pursues are mini marquetry versions in tortoise and horn, sized to slip into a vest pocket.

Though the trove is almost a hundred strong, the containers are so small they fit in a petite collector's cabinet.

A dresser top becomes a shrine-like cabinet of curiosities when layered with a collection of VOODOO SOUVENIRS, most of them Mayan and Peruvian. These quirky fetish objects, fashioned as talismans to ward off evil spirits, also make for great conversation pieces.

This collector loves DICE of all sizes, colors, and materials, from tiny Bakelite and Lucite ones to overscaled versions made of wood, ceramic, metal, or vinyl-covered foam. The display suggests controlled insanity: The dice fill a bookcase in his living area, spilling over onto the floor and an adjacent side table.

His smaller collectibles, stored in a tabletop vitrine, are similarly diverse in design and material, from plastic to glass. The making of GAME PIECES was a popular amateur craft often executed by sailors; antique versions are commonly fabricated of animal bone or crudely carved wood.

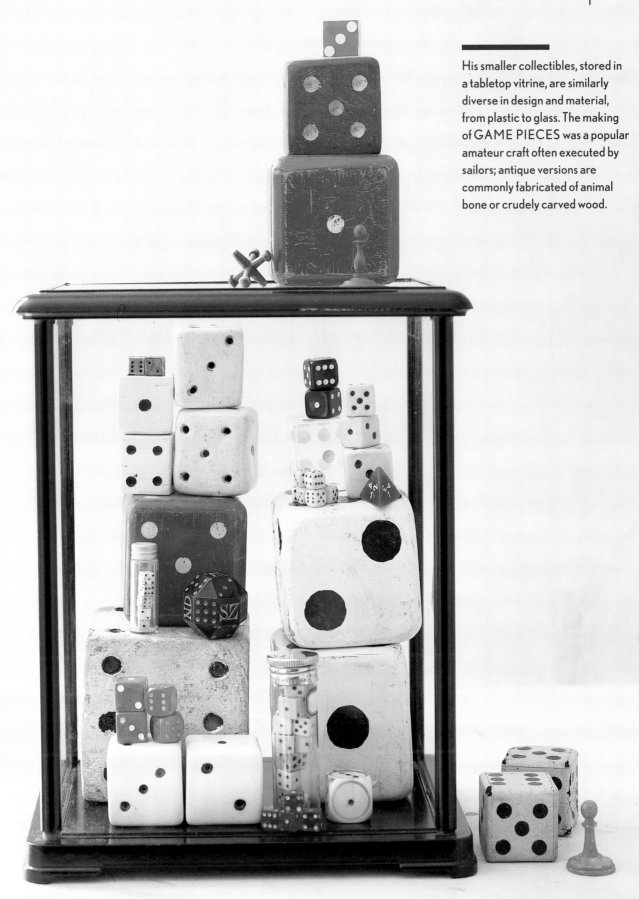

MANY COLLECTORS EMBRACE EXTREMES of scale, whether gargantuan or petite. Miniaturists fall decidedly into the latter camp. They have outsize zeal for undersize things: doll furniture and little snuffboxes, dwarfish baskets and Cracker Jack charms. The miniaturist is subconsciously (at times irrationally) drawn to the Lilliputian. How else to explain the enthusiasm that otherwise sensible people have for itty-bitty oil cans—a surprisingly common miniaturist obsession?

There's just something charming in the translation of an object, no matter how mundane, into a tiny version of itself—it becomes whimsical and irresistibly appealing. Miniaturism also inspires wonderment and admiration when one

Produced in early nineteenth-century England, CERAMIC CALICO BUTTONS were decorated via a transferware process. Accordingly, the fabric-inspired embellishments came in the same colors as transferware tabletop items: brown, blue, green, and reddish pink. Most were made for kids' clothes, hence their supersmall size. Even antique versions are relatively easy to find and often affordably priced, making the genre a fun collectible.

considers the masterful level of craft that the execution of weensy things entails: writing the Lord's Prayer on the head of a pin, chiseling millimeter-thick dovetail joints on the drawers of dollhouse furniture. It takes great skill and finesse to fabricate such minutiae—from the workmanship and the tools to the inventiveness required to scale down.

The miniaturist's desire for the diminutive can appear wholeheartedly fanciful; after all, an inch-high chinoiserie vase is more objet d'art than functional object. But pursuing minuscule forms is this collector's way of being pragmatic. Wee treasures can be accumulated in abundance yet easily tucked away. Fifty travel chess sets will fit in a single drawer; a thousand calico buttons might fill a shoebox. Miniaturism is thus an ideal strategy for small-house dwellers or the storage-strapped. And indeed, square-footage constraints are often the driver: Downsizing from a four-bedroom home to a studio apartment, a devotee of modernist chairs may switch to collecting minute versions instead. Kids are frequently miniaturists, because they physically relate to smaller-scale items and have limited space to call their own.

Teeny-tiny trinkets take up less room—and less mental energy. Because the chaos can be readily contained, the collection doesn't overwhelm their home or life the way the maximalist's menagerie sometimes does. Thinking small allows miniaturists to have a controlled compulsion, one that can be hidden from the world if desired. Who will ever know if you own three hundred salt spoons? While many people love sharing their passions with

others, there are those who consider collecting to be a private act for personal enjoyment. Smallness enables secrecy.

Financial constraints often impel miniaturism. A model yacht is certainly more affordable than the real thing; a rinky-dink chair costs a fraction the price of a full-size one. The miniaturist can spend an entire afternoon trolling vintage shops and flea markets, drop just thirty dollars, and add five new things to their collection—all of which fit in their tote bag. (Or their carry-on: Miniaturism is popular among frequent flyers.) Collectors of vintage lamps or antique rug beaters do not have such a luxury.

Miniaturists have grand ambitions. They aspire to utter comprehensiveness within their chosen genre—one of every style button ever produced. The goal isn't mass accumulation but encyclopedic variety. Collectors of full-size pitchers generally gravitate to one subset—ironstone, for instance—whereas miniaturists chase the entire universe of possibilities.

Dollhouses are, of course, another favorite of the miniaturist. For many adults, styling these undersize residences was their childhood entrée into the world of design and decor and, indeed, to collecting. A dollhouse is both a secret fantasy world and a portal into its creator's mind—a microcosm of his or her imagination and of the manifold domestic delights the material world offers.

Buttons are a fun pursuit: They are ubiquitous, affordable, and about as small as anything you can possibly collect. Troll through the BUTTON BOX at any estate sale and you'll likely find a few gems. This trove is a veritable history of material techniques, including enamel, mother-of-pearl, metalwork, ceramic transferware, and Bakelite.

Nested MIXING BOWLS—like
these early 1900s American
yellow-ware versions—were a staple
of farmhouse kitchens back in the
day. For aficionados, the largest
and smallest of the set are the most
prized; the tiniest is equivalent to
one cup and were often used as
measuring scoops.

Because of their small size, miniatures can be challenging to display, getting a bit lost in the context of a human-sized home. Here, diminutive 1970s-STYLE FURNISHINGS are arrayed in a glass-enclosed vintage bakery case—with its shelves removed—a fun twist on a traditional dollhouse, and a humorous riff on Phillip Johnson's modernist Glass House.

THIS PAGE A horde of PAPER CLIPS celebrates the sheer variety within this one utilitarian category, and offers a window onto human ingenuity: There are so many ways to achieve the very same goal of attaching two pieces of paper. The collection encompasses examples from all over the world and in myriad formats, from the familiar oblong ellipse to "owl" clips and butterfly clamps, as well as figural motifs.

OPPOSITE Organized in militant rows on white paper like a science specimen, this menagerie of vintage clips is likely a SALESMAN'S CARD, used to show off the full spectrum of one factory's wares to clients.

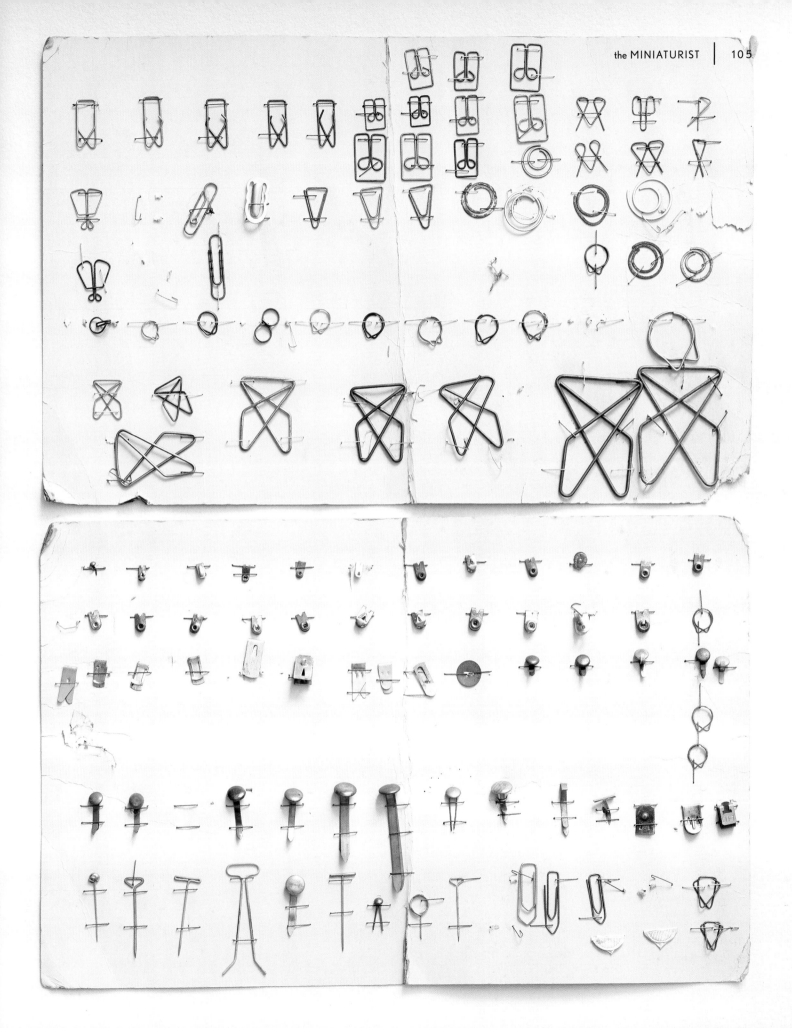

OPPOSITE A parade of WEE PITCHERS lines a kitchen windowsill—an ideal place to display small curios. Juxtaposed with full-size versions, they look especially petite. Though the collection exhibits a broad array of global ethnic craft—from Mediterranean glassware to South American pottery—it nonetheless fits into a shoebox.

THIS PAGE Mini pitchers sit atop a TINY TABLE (actually a traveling salesman's scaled-down sample); below is a small-sized creamer. The vessels, in red earthenware, glazed ceramic, and glass, were made for dollhouses or as collectibles. It was a technical tour de force for a master craftsman to blow a glass pitcher on such a diminutive scale.

DON'T RELEGATE SPECIAL SPOONS TO
THE SILVERWARE DRAWER! A LARGE FLAT-
BOTTOMED BOWL OR TRAY, LIKE THIS PEWTER
CHARGER, MAKES AN INSPIRED DISPLAY
PEDESTAL—WHILE CREATING AN ARTFUL
METAL-ON-METAL MOMENT.

1d. Mauve

7 – 12

19 – 24

31 – 36

43 –48

55 – 60

67 – 72

79 –84

91 – 96

103 –108

115 –120

Krb Setting
Upper Right Pane

OPPOSITE Many of these TEENSY SPOONS were designed for master or individual salt dishes. Like sugar, salt was super-expensive in the eighteenth century—a time when households would keep it under lock and key, lest servants dip into the stash—and the wealthy would serve it in a huge bowl as a covetous presentation of abundance. Later, in the Victorian era, when the seasoning became more accessible and mealtime rituals more codified, each dinner guest would have their own salt cellar, accompanied by a dainty spoon for dispensing.

THIS PAGE Stamp collecting is a popular passion for many miniaturists, but this collection is a bit rarefied. In the late 1800s, the New Zealand Post and Telegraph Department released a series of stamps whose sticky side was PRINTED WITH ADS for grocery items: Poneke Table Jelly, Crease's Dandelion Coffee Cures. They were wildly unpopular during their day, as the inks used to print the ads rendered the stamps inadequately tacky—and consumers disliked being bombarded with advertising.

In the mid-nineteenth century, it didn't suffice to hang art on a plain nail. Like everything else in the Victorian era, even the mundane was fancified: A decorative PICTURE NAIL was the preferred device. Like jewelry for the wall, they were bedecked with gems, ribbons, or tassels. In the same vein are tiebacks for window treatments, and mirror hooks—also called mirror knobs—which lent looking glasses appropriate pomp. This collection is doubly witty: framed picture nails are hung with . . . yes, picture nails.

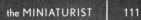

Every crafter of a certain era had
a sewing kit complete with a
HOMEMADE PINCUSHION,
many in the form of a fruit or insect.
Most common were tomatoes,
accompanied by a strawberry-
shaped needle sharpener. They
were often made from fabric scraps
as little gifts for Mom.

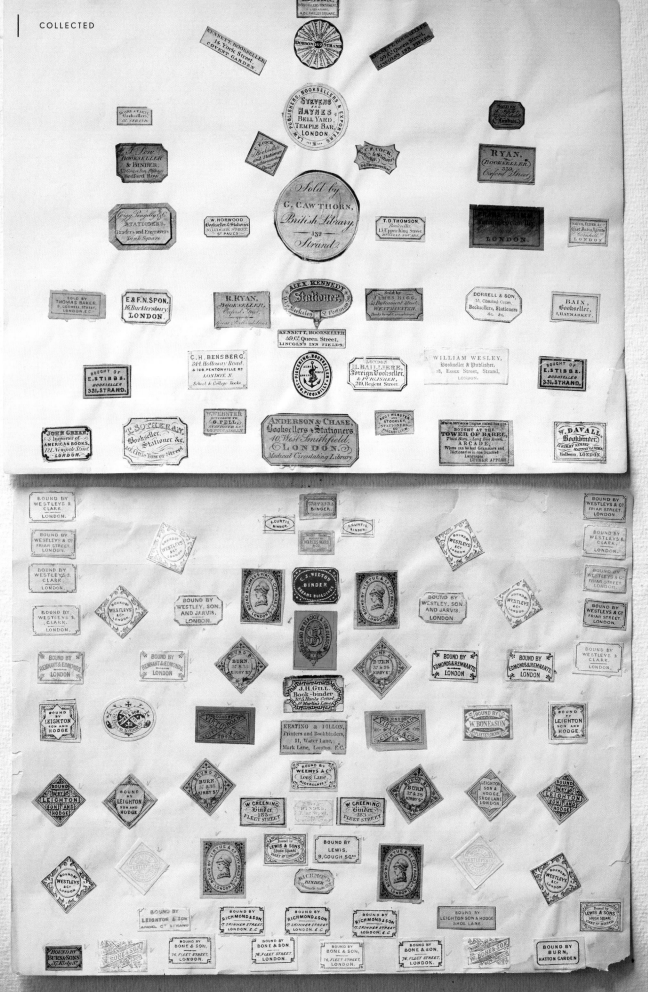

OPPOSITE A collection of eighteenth- and nineteenth-century BOOKSELLER'S LABELS is mounted to white paper and organized by city, from London to Manchester. Each seller had their own logo design as a sort of branding stamp.

THIS PAGE American Indian tribes from Maine made elaborate WOVEN CREATIONS for the tourist market, including this tableau of sewing items: itty-bitty baskets for holding buttons, needle cases, pincushions, and scissor holders. Basket weaving on such a minute scale was an extremely advanced skill. Note the mini sewing basket at bottom right, from whose lid dangles even tinier versions housing thimbles.

While it's rare today to receive a formal document kissed with a wax seal, the practice was common from the medieval period through the nineteenth century. Too lovely to toss, the signature-like impressions were often saved. Motifs ranged from cameos and monograms to cartouches and crests, and the wax came in every color of the rainbow.

A common practice of the more advanced, ambitious connoisseur is to purchase pre-existing collections of favorite objects—thus benefiting from the efforts of a previous generation. Among this miniaturist's WAX-SEAL holdings are an entire bound volume assembled by a single curatorial eye a century ago. Indeed, it wouldn't even be possible to form such a collection today, given the obsolescence of the seals; even if you found one on an ancient document, it would be too brittle to peel off. Collections of stamps and coins similarly get disassembled and re-cataloged over the decades.

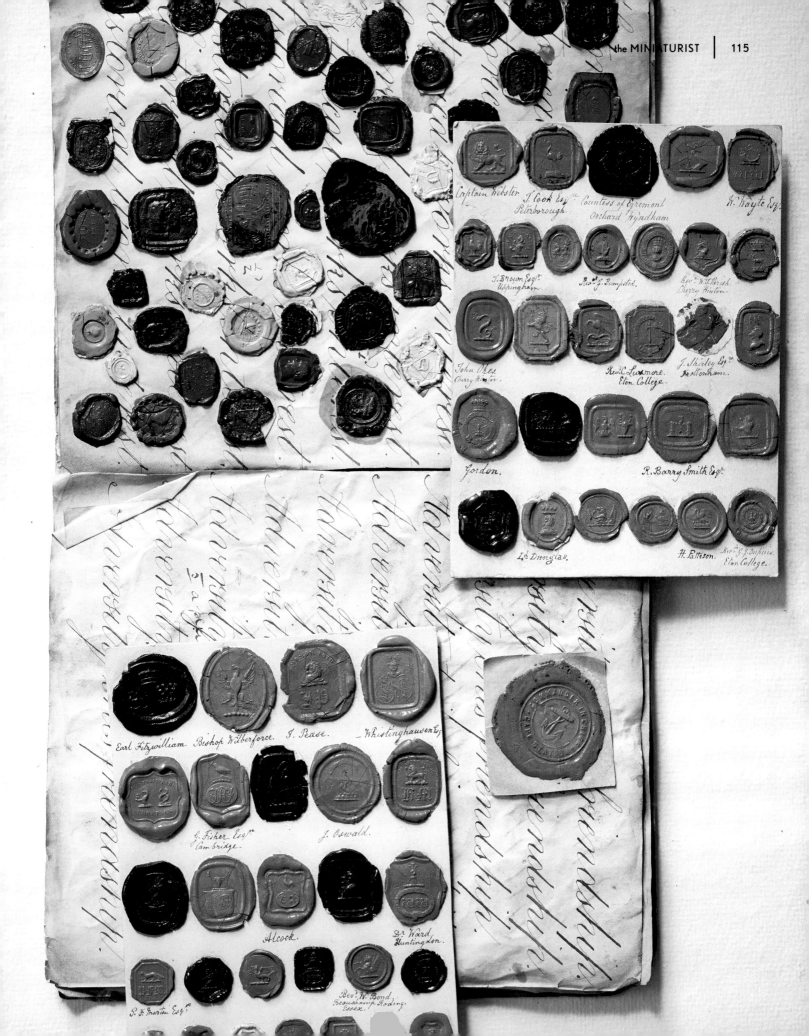

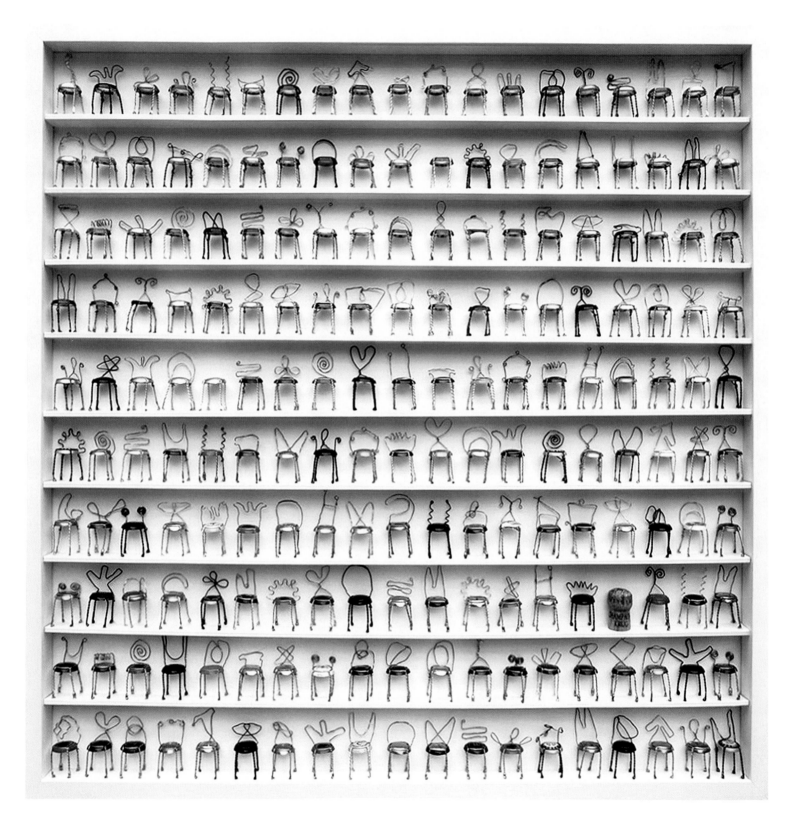

OPPOSITE **A collection of bubbly chairs fabricated from twisted and CURLICUED CHAMPAGNE CORKS** neatly displays the degree of ingenuity that can be applied to a humble disposable. These delicacies were all made by Joanne Tinker, a London-based contemporary artist, who showcases them en masse in an appropriately tiny shelving unit.

THIS PAGE This miniaturist collects early **CRACKER JACK PRIZES** which she strings onto exuberant necklaces; her holdings number in the thousands. Charms from the 1920s and 1930s are most coveted, as they're elaborately detailed and made from metal, not plastic. (Childhood nostalgia often fuels this obsession.)

This miniaturist once collected full-size chairs, but after cohabitating with many dozen in a studio apartment, he realized it was time to downsize—literally. Now he accumulates MINIATURE MODELS (and tiny tables, too). He is especially drawn to amateur homemade furnishings, which exhibit a charming, slightly off sense of scale and were commonly whittled from Popsicle sticks and repurposed cigar boxes.

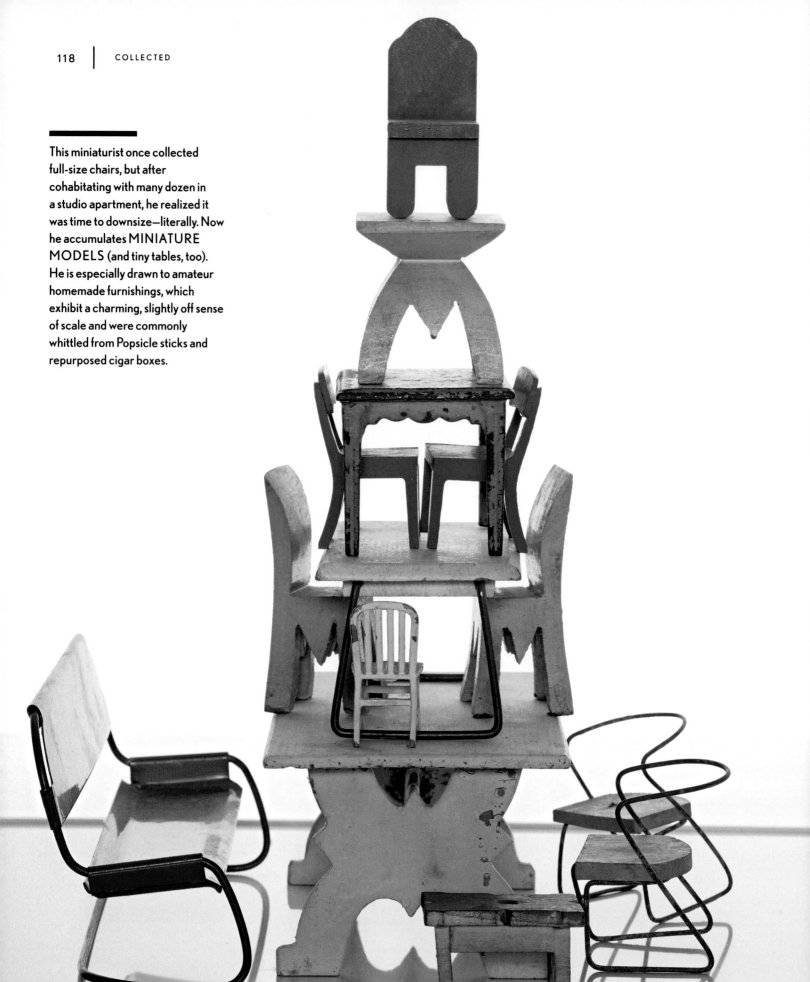

An argument for forgoing a
traditional dollhouse structure:
The pint-size furnishings create a
WHIMSICAL TABLESCAPE,
propped up on books employed as
de facto display pedestals.

After inheriting an early 1900s Scottish Arts & Crafts dollhouse, the new owner lovingly restored it and then redecorated it in period-appropriate style including William Morris–inspired furniture. The cottage is now filled to the gills with all manner of furnishings, tchotchkes, and pets—a delightfully lifelike mirror of the collector's own abode.

THIS PAGE The facade of the ARTS & CRAFTS COTTAGE is clad in wooden shingles. Among the owner's many upgrades were a restored roof and modernized electrical system—just like a real-life home renovation.

OPPOSITE You have to look twice to realize that this is a DOLLHOUSE KITCHEN, not a life-sized one. It's been lavished with such detail, fantasy, and verisimilitude—down to the transferware turkey platter on the wall, the open cookbooks, and the jar of herb-infused olive oil.

Another inspired alternative to a dollhouse: The same collector maintains a meticulously restored and decorated model cabin cruiser of 1920s vintage; she calls it her "GATSBY PICNIC BOAT." The deck vignette is obsessively detailed, complete with fruit-based cocktails and a tray of deviled eggs.

The CABIN CRUISER is the size of a dollhouse, extending four and a half feet long. While model boats are common on the vintage market, most are yachts; it's rare to encounter a pleasure picnicking boat.

YOU DON'T NEED
SPECIALIZED FURNISHINGS
TO SHOWCASE PRIZED
POSSESSIONS—EVEN A
DRESSER TOP WILL SUFFICE.

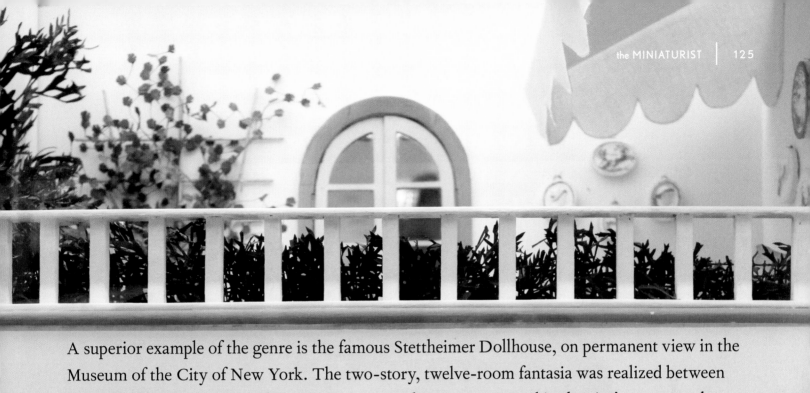

A superior example of the genre is the famous Stettheimer Dollhouse, on permanent view in the Museum of the City of New York. The two-story, twelve-room fantasia was realized between 1916 and 1935 by Carrie Stettheimer, an eccentric heiress. Immersed in the city's avant-garde scene, she and her two sisters commissioned their artist friends to create little works for the house. Among other masterpieces are cubist paintings, a Gaston Lachaise nude, and a sculpture by Alexander Archipenko.

The dollhouse took the form of a sophisticated URBAN TOWN HOUSE, complete with an art-filled loggia, service spaces like a pantry and laundry boudoir, and even an elevator. This personal little fanatasy world was more about charm and artistry than about capturing a particular period décor, as was the case with most dollhouses.

OBSESSIVELY COLLECTING objects by hue, the colorist lives in vivid, saturated splendor. Driven by palette, they are drawn to a particular shade or color combination. Unlike many collectors, the colorist is unconcerned with value, vintage, and uniqueness; they're more interested in the sum of the parts, the effect of the whole, the frisson they get from viewing shelves stacked with all-red books. Taken on its own, each piece in their collection may not be so compelling, but viewed together, arranged by color family, they make a dramatic, chromatic impact. Color is this collector's primary motivator and the impetus behind their decorating style. It's also a sanity-leveler, helping them narrow their choices in an abundant world.

Some colorists obsess over a single hue; others collect just one object—like CONVERSE ALL STARS—but in every conceivable colorway. So powerful is the effect of color that a rainbow of sneakers tucked in a closet becomes a form of installation art.

The most common type of colorist collects varied objects in a single hue: anything green, *anything pink*! Said color may be quite specific—traceable to a Pantone chip—or shades within a spectrum. They live in a tonal or tone-on-tone fantasy, their interior a forest of green or sea of cerulean and white—from throw pillows to Chinese ginger jars. Some colorists go for bolder combinations like orange/purple or red/black spiked with gray, and thread them through every room. The look is utterly cohesive (if a tad totalizing).

Other colorists gravitate to a favorite shade within a particular product category: citron typewriters or Turkey red tablecloths, for instance. These collectors display their belongings like art installations: kitting out a glass-front cabinet with lavender decanters, accenting a sitting area with an array of red lacquerware. A third type of colorist collects a single genre—often something commonplace, like sneakers or knitting needles—but in a joyous spectrum of hues. They group items by color or in a happy polychrome mélange.

Color has strong associations. Red bespeaks passion; yellow signifies madness. And red plus yellow stimulates the appetite, hence the combination's popularity for tabletop items. Such connotations often inform personal color preference, and so does regional climate. In England, for instance, where non-summer months are gray, there exists a predilection for acid hues. That same palette prevails in the Caribbean for the opposite reason: Year-round, the weather's so bright that less-saturated colors look washed out. The Scandinavian sensibility is a defense against limited daylight: White and watercolor-pastel hues paired with shimmery metallics amplify the scant sunshine.

Historically, certain colors also conveyed status or rarity. In Persia, green belonged to the sultan alone; thus its notable absence from antique Persian carpets. Similarly, yellow was reserved for the emperor in imperial China. Other hues, like indigo and cobalt, derive from precious commodities and were accordingly exorbitant. Nineteenth-century ruby glass, for instance, gets its distinctive jewel tone from melted gold, now too pricey to use for common articles.

Indeed, the purity and richness of color found in vintage items is unsurpassed today, especially by mass-market products. In vintage objects, coloration derived from natural processes, extracted from plants and minerals (many of them rare or extinct); there was a connection to the raw material. In contrast, modern dyes and pigments are cooked up in the chemistry lab and have less integrity and presence. Which touches on an important point: A material's character and finish—whether glossy or matte, translucent or opaque, applied or integral—affects our perception of its color. The red of ruby glass is different than that of red Pyrex. Blue-tinted metal and blue-dyed textiles are likewise distinct. Because of this, colorists will often gravitate not just to a specific shade but that shade rendered in a specific material.

The following collections inspire and inform on many levels. They suggest the many ways color can be used as a springboard for interior design, whether to instill cohesion or create harmonious arrangements. Color has abundant historical and symbolic value, but it can serve strictly aesthetic purposes, too: to brighten, to calm, to invigorate, to soothe, to transport, and to please.

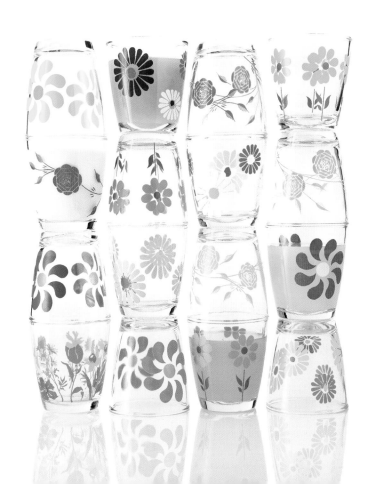

Bright and bold objects are catnip to colorists. Take these juice tumblers, actually vintage SOUR CREAM JARS. After the Great Depression, food makers lured shoppers with pert packaging that doubled as a giveaway. At the time, the dairy industry was dominated by local producers. Although most purchased stock designs from glassworks, larger distributors could afford to commission custom colors and patterns—hence the variety you'll discover.

Like a bowerbird, this collector flocks to primary colors and catchy hues, from aqua to orange. Among her polychromatic possessions are mod post-war SCANDINAVIAN ENAMELWARE, including Dansk coffeepots and prized lotus-leaf-patterned plates and bowls by erstwhile Norwegian producer Cathrineholm. She purchased the vintage pieces exclusively from thrift shops and other budget-friendly sources—a feat complicated by the category's rising popularity (and soaring price points).

THIS PAGE Crimson WATERING CANS frame a garden view, inviting the outdoors in (a job that's usually reserved for verdant green). The pick-me-up hue brings a cheery note to the kitchen—and a dose of whimsy to a utilitarian object.

OPPOSITE Collecting by color transforms the mundane into the magical. A full spectrum of KNITTING NEEDLES organized by hue upgrades this ensemble.

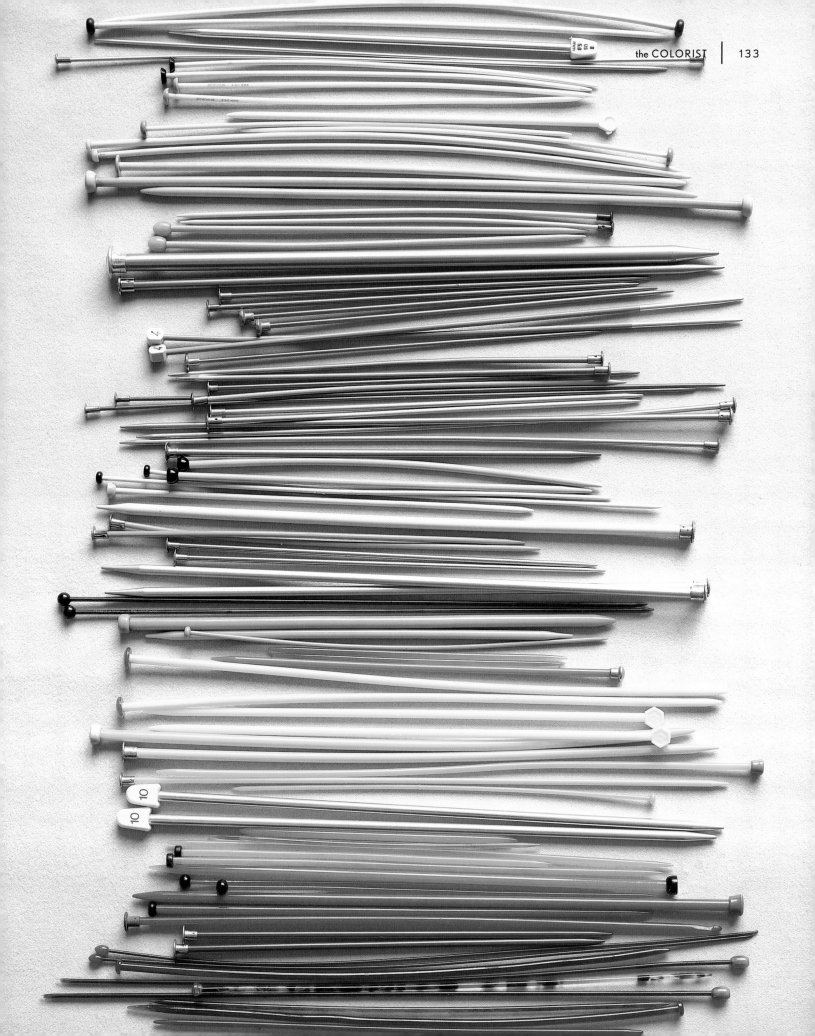

OPPOSITE Many colorists are seduced by the allure of enamel, a material that's been produced continuously for centuries in many countries—and in myriad hues. This collector has an eye for ENAMELWARE COFFEEPOTS, from antique to modern, but only in fire-engine red. Made of steel coated with vitreous porcelain enamel, the material maintains its sultry pigmentation over time.

THIS PAGE An abundance of enamelware begs to be displayed, not stored away. Wall-hung POTS AND PANS make for a spirited decorative accent that's user-friendly, too. And while conventional wisdom suggests backdropping a boldly hued collection with a light-toned neutral, color-on-color proved a more sophisticated strategy here. The strong, dark green stands up to the red while tempering its intensity.

The Lincoln, Massachusetts, home of architect Walter Gropius and his wife, Ise, was a showpiece of modernist design and Bauhaus furnishings. Drama was achieved through striking forms while colors were primarily kept to neutral, earth-toned hues. The main accent color was red, a shade that animates MRS. GROPIUS' VANITY, accessorized with tokens of the couple's world travels (a luxury they embraced after escaping Nazi Germany for America).

THIS PAGE Opaline glass is opaque, resulting in a much greater intensity of color than can be found in translucent varieties. Made in smoldering hues like violet, turquoise, jade, and rare pink, the material has a pure, crisp coloration. OPALINE was complicated to fabricate, accounting for its short life span: It was produced in France for less than a century, beginning in the early 1800s.

OPPOSITE When he moved into his 1960s modernist apartment, in a Miami high-rise by Morris Lapidus, this design maven set out to preserve the PERIOD VIBE. In the kitchen, that meant keeping the original appliances and carnation-pattern floor tiles, purchasing mid-century finds like the Eero Saarinen–esque dining set, and drenching walls in sixties-appropriate turquoise.

MATTRESS TICKING typically comes in combinations of white with blue or red (although in the 1960s it was possible to buy versions with lime green, orange, or yellow stripes). Ideal for repurposing into craft projects, the material takes dye well. Snip piece to size and treat to bold colors or more natural vegetal dyes. Although the material has a canvas-like feel when new, it softens over time into a texture that's perfect for pillows and quilts.

Chinaware collecting blossomed in the nineteenth century, and landscapes are among the most popular patterns. Consumers treated these pieces like paintings, a window to a faraway place and time—the more exotic the better in an era when international travel was severely limited.

Get creative and exploit vertical surfaces as display—not only walls but the insides of window frames, too. An assemblage of blue-and-white ceramic pieces, including centuries-old DELFT TILE SEASCAPES and chinoiserie landscape platters, lends an antiquarian aura while the common colorway and motif bestow unity.

An assortment of honey-toned objects is corralled in a grid of boxlike shelving. COLOR BLOCKING is a stylist's favorite trick, defining a spatial zone—whether a tabletop or shelf—with a continuous swath of hue. It's an especially effective and easy-to-pull-off look for anyone who collects by color palette.

Enamored with the variety of colors and patterns that quotidian CAFÉ AU LAIT bowls came in, this collector has amassed more than 150 so far, most scored abroad on French eBay and other European markets.

THIS PAGE Some dishware mavens hone in on a particular maker, like Sèvres or Meissen; others favor a subject matter, like fruit, botanicals, or landscapes. Colorists, naturally, are drawn to a palette. Displayed on plate stands or wall-mounted like little artworks, these GRISAILLE SCENES stand out against earthy pink plaster.

OPPOSITE Made in the town of Sunderland, England in the early 1800s and revived a century later, festive LUSTERWARE came in a marbleized pastel-pink hue. The coloration is acheived via chemicals in the glaze that react to heat, turning pink in a lower-temperature kiln—and darkening to copper if subject to higher temperatures.

A bounteous cluster of GLASS VESSELS tells a history of the material's techniques and forms—from jars to aquariums—and demonstrates the primal power of color. Glass is composed of minerals melted with local sand; accordingly, color varied slightly depending on where the glass was made—not unlike the way terroir affects the taste of wine. Russian glass has a yellow tint, New Jersey a beautiful aqua. Glass was made all over the globe, but the most skilled makers were English, Bohemian, and Irish artisans, many of whom immigrated to America over the centuries.

OVERSIZED GLASS
VESSELS ARE IDEAL
FOR INJECTING
COLOR AND LIGHT
INTO A ROOM.

OPPOSITE An extreme version of the colorist is one who collects even the most quotidian odds and ends in a specific hue—quite literally collecting a color, not a thing. A whitewashed loft is accented with PUNCHES OF CRIMSON; even the pantry area, stacked with all manner of red bric-a-brac, is color coordinated.

THIS PAGE The softer side of crimson: TURKEY RED TEXTILES. The color is made via a laborious colorfast dye process that originated in the Middle East (hence the name). The cloths—typically bordered table coverings—were woven on a damask loom that created a reverse of the pattern on the backside. Quilts, blankets, shawls, and other textiles bring a shock of color and pattern to a room, whether spread out on a table or bed, folded over the arm of a sofa, or draped on chair backs.

Still found on eBay for a song, these pretty PYREX storage containers can go from oven to table to fridge, making a saturated statement during mealtime. The super-durable borosilicate glass was invented by Corning in 1915. But it wasn't until 1947 that the company began producing the ovenware in colors, substituting borosilicate with soda lime (which made it stronger to boot) and fusing paint to white milk glass. In its heyday, the glassware came in more than fifteen colorways.

Bakelite became a collecting obsession in the 1980s. The early synthetic plastic was made of phenolic resin and, in addition to industrial applications, was crafted into jewelry and decorative accents. BAKELITE-HANDLED FLATWARE was especially ubiquitous and came in solid hues or inlaid with patterns in a contrasting color or colors. The polychromatic versions are the Holy Grail for Bakelite enthusiasts. Children's versions are especially charming and elusive, decorated with whimsical imagery like bunny rabbits and Scottie dogs.

THERE'S A SUBLIMINAL ASPECT TO COLOR, CONJURING THE YOUTHFUL FANTASY OF A CANDY STORE (AND HAPPINESS). IS IT ANY COINCIDENCE THAT BAKELITE RED IS THE SAME COLOR AS RED LICORICE?

WHEREAS COLORISTS ENVELOP themselves in joyous, contrasting hues, neutralists favor the visual quiet of a muted palette. The colorist craves stimulation; the neutralist, tranquility. Averse to brights, allergic to strong color shifts, such collectors outfit their homes in calming creams, washed-out whites, or layered shades of gray and brown.

The neutralist's yen for subdued hues plays out in two ways. First, they tend to collect items that are spare in coloration, often made of natural materials like clay or metal. Obsessions include milk glass, turned-wood pepper mills, mid-century-modern porcelain, and ceramic pitchers—items whose living finish fades or darkens with time and wear. The neutralist has a keen eye for patina, embracing signs of age like peeling paint, verdigris metals, and sun-bleached linens.

Collectors of mid-century WEST GERMAN POTTERY tend to go for vases and vessels glazed fiery orange and crimson. These white porcelain wonders are just as flamboyant, yet still somewhat minimalist—a meditation on shape and surface texture.

Second, neutralism governs this collector's overarching approach to décor and display. A medley of hushed surfaces—grass-cloth wall covering, greige upholstery, raw concrete floors—creates a quiet backdrop, one that lets the neutralist live with more (and more eclectic) objects. Even the most overstuffed room never looks too busy when rendered in white-on-white. Additionally, a pale environment puts the focus on the forms and silhouettes of the objects and furnishings within; everything looks more sculptural in a low-contrast context. The intricate weaving of Native American baskets, the convex dimples of copper food molds—such details really pop when there's an absence of strong color to distract the eye.

Collecting items within a disciplined palette also draws out the super-subtle distinctions between near-identical objects. A set of ironstone platters, each aged to a slightly different shade of cream, looks like a rainbow of hues. A grouping of pewter pitchers invites comparison between profiles; as your eye lingers, it starts to notice how the mottling varies in pattern and intensity from piece to piece.

The neutral approach to collecting and decorating is both time-honored and trendy. Famous practitioners of neutralism include the Scandinavians, especially during the Gustavian period, and the Shakers. In more recent decades, a tone-on-tone scheme has become one of the most dominant decorating tropes. It used to be that the prototypical antiquarian embraced bold color and energetic pairings: high-shine French-polish mahogany furniture set against bright, happy hues like light blue or yellow, anchored with vibrant Persian carpets and accessorized with ruby-red cranberry glass. Sweeping in from Paris and Antwerp like a cool, calming breeze in the 1980s was an aesthetic of chalky textures, pale linens, worn-in woods, and galvanized steel garden furnishings brought indoors. The vogue for neutral, unsaturated rooms, accented with a hit of metallics and vintage industrial ephemera, has sparked the popularity of simpatico collecting categories like drabware and basalt Wedgwood.

It's important to distinguish between monochrome and monotone. When executed with a light touch and appropriate nuance, a neutral scheme is anything but one-note. Even within a reduced palette there's ample room for visual variety. Contrast can come from juxtaposition of texture—a sophisticated play between shiny and matte, smooth and variegated, honed and satiny. For collectors of every stripe, a neutral palette is an ideal strategy, because it makes everything look cohesive and allows for easy rearrangement. It creates a calm stage not only for collections but also for life. Nothing neutral about that.

OPPOSITE Primarily produced in nineteenth-century England, super-thin hand-blown BRISTOL GLASS was opaque yet translucent. Whereas its close cousin, opaline glass, was often made in sweet pastels that mimicked Peking glass, Bristol glass came in more muted hues. The glassware was generally highly embellished with enameling, handpainting, or giltwork that faded over time; for a more restrained look in keeping with contemporary tastes, collectors (and dealers) often wash off or otherwise remove the decorations.

THIS PAGE White-on-white looks restful, not overly slick, when given a textural boost. A collection of quilted MATELASSÉ BEDSPREADS was transformed into decorative treatments, draped over a tabletop and cladding lampshades, a decorative box, and even the wall.

Vintage baskets bring an earthy note to any interior. This collection of woven whimsies was crafted by Native Americans. Tribes such as the Penobscot and Mackinac made one style of basket for their own use, and showier, more exuberant designs for the tourist trade. Each maker had a signature style, often favoring highly dimensional surfaces.

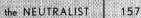

GRASS-CLOTH WALL
COVERING AND
WEATHERED-WOOD
SURFACES REINFORCE
THE SOOTHING PLAY
OF TEXTURE.

OPPOSITE Native American basket designs were quite fanciful, even figurative. Here, woven LOOP-DE-LOOPS and CUT SPLINTS mimic the seeds and stem of a strawberry. The baskets were often painted or dyed in bright colors, which dulled over time; sometimes you'll open a lid to find the original hues intact.

THIS PAGE Mirroring the warm beige-brown tones of the NATURAL FIBERS are small wooden stools and tables, serving as display pedestals to create a skyline of baskets. Grouping the baskets together invites comparison between the weave patterns and shapes

The term DRABWARE—which described a colorway rather than a particular type of ceramic—is something of a misnomer: The nineteenth-century English pottery exhibits somewhat spirited neutral hues ranging from camel and straw to green and gray-brown. Unified by an even, matte tone, a family of drabware and molded stoneware pitchers lends muted intrigue to a dining room.

THIS TABLEAU IS A
TONE POEM OF PATINA—
THE WORN PITCHERS,
WEATHERED CUPBOARD,
THE PLASTER WALL FADED
TO A PAINTERLY SHEEN.

A collection of trays designed for drying fruit and seeds makes an elemental statement in a kitchen; galvanized steel ages beautifully, oxidizing over time into a PAINTERLY GRADATION OF GRAYS. The practical and sturdy material was also used for serving trays in environments like prisons, hospitals, churches, firehouses, and mess halls where durability was essential.

Though they look like typical pen-and-ink drawings, these grisaille artworks are executed in marble dust. The process involved brushing a pasteboard substrate with adhesive and then sprinkling a fine layer of marble dust on top. After the surface dried, the artist would sketch in charcoal. Sometimes called monochromatic paintings or sandpaper drawings, the medium became popular in the mid-1800s as a precursor to photography. This collector owns many versions of the same landscape scene.

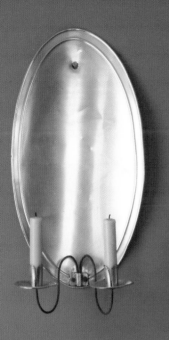

This dining vignette has the mysterious aura and moody coloration of a Vermeer painting. The lichen-hued wall paint is offset by touches of rose-toned metals: a Colonial-revival sconce in copper, a spun-brass compote, nineteenth-century English lusterware, and a pair of 1960s brass chairs by Gio Ponti.

OFFSET A COLLECTION OF METALLIC OBJECTS WITH DARK, MATTE SURROUNDINGS TO ESTABLISH AN INTERPLAY OF SOFT AND SHIMMERY. OR GO FOR THE OPPOSITE EFFECT, LAYERING SHINE ON SHINE.

Copper pudding molds may be functional kitchen tools, but carefully curated in abundant rows they look like sculptures (or stylized wedding cakes). ANTIQUE MOLDS, of which there is abundant variety, are highly collectible, beloved for their comely forms and sultry shimmer. Copper versions were especially coveted at their time, too, and are often found monogrammed with the family crest or bedecked with a number that signified its place in the kitchen inventory. The desserts they created were deployed as confectionary centerpieces at mealtime.

The same limited palette of colors and finishes can vary greatly depending on how it comes together. WHITE HUES and WEATHERED WOODS can veer from earthy or ethereal; here, they strike a glam, polished note with the infusion of abstract art and high-shine metals.

As strong as porcelain, ironstone was the most utilitarian and basic of pottery, a fixture of farmhouses—as well as every hospital, cafeteria, and hotels of a certain eras. Shaker households often had them in the plainest profiles (and in wide size variance). Over time, the pure white coloration fades to manifold hues, from ecru to butterscotch, and develops painterly splotches. The subtle variegation, coupled with the soft tones of the room, gives this tableau a Zen-like, contemplative quality.

STYLE TIP: HANG PLATES, PLATTERS, AND OTHER COLLECTIBLES IN A TELESCOPING INSTALLATION FROM LARGE TO SMALL.

OPPOSITE **One of this collecting couple's many fixations is** WEDGWOOD BASALT **coffee and teapots, showcased as objets d'art on their cocktail table. The pottery's matte black hue is complemented by neutral surroundings, from charcoal-colored couches to ivory walls and golden-toned woods.**

THIS PAGE **Wedgwood first produced the inky-black** STONEWARE **in 1786. The coloration comes from the firing process: Manganese added to brown clay turns obsidian when exposed to heat.**

This author/collector literally wrote the book on modernist pepper mills. One wall of his home is a shrine to the works of Danish industrial designer (and self-taught craftsman) Jens Quistgaard, who envisioned lathe-turned TEAK PEPPER MILLS for Dansk. These curvaceous implements were ubiquitous in the mid-century and helped introduce Danish modern to an American audience. The collector's salon-style presentation technique is a twenty-first-century version of the traditional china cabinet, each pepper mill perched on its own shelf.

THIS PAGE Throw pillows are a fun and easy crafting project, and a wonderful way to bring a collection of antique cloths to life. This collector scoured the web for VINTAGE FASHION SCARVES by Norell, Vera, and other labels—all in the same black-and-white palette. Backed and sewn into oversize pillows, they offer a tonal but graphic look.

OPPOSITE Bought new, a 32-inch-square pillow can be pricey; a homemade version fashioned from vintage scarves costs very little—leaving enough cash in your wallet to start a whole new collection. Another advantage of DIY THROW PILLOWS: a completely custom, one-of-a-kind accent.

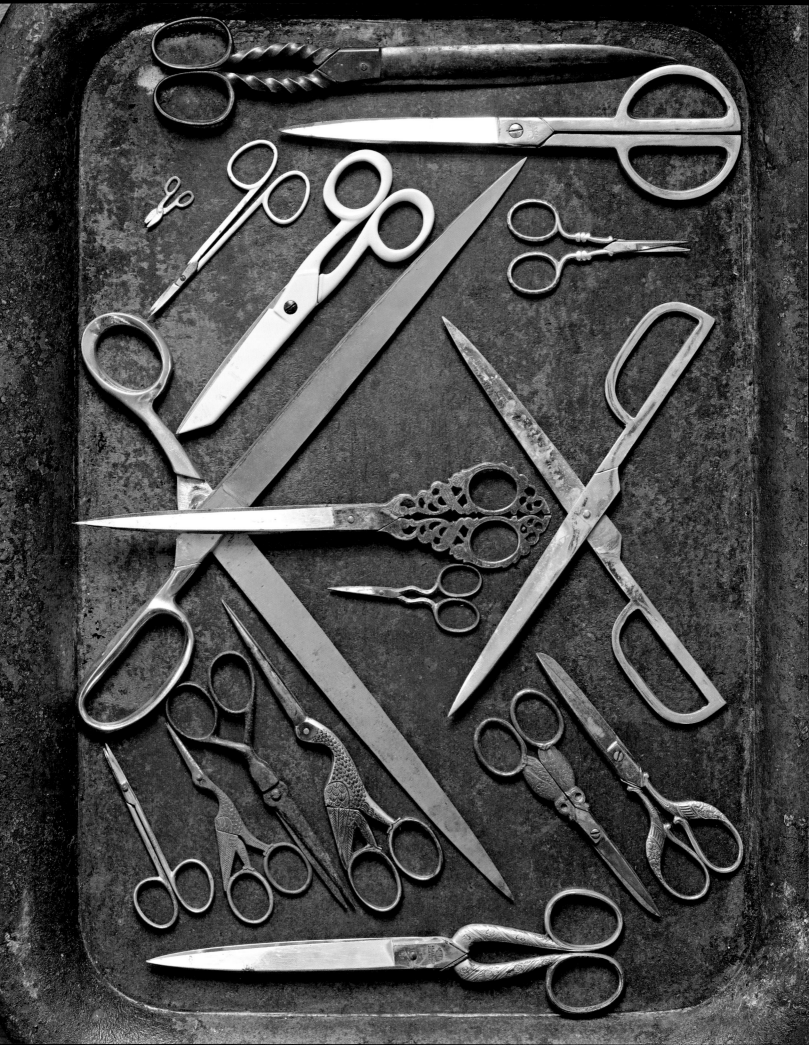

MECHANICAL OBJECTS AND OBSOLETE technologies are what make this collector tick. A connoisseur of mid-century clocks, early handheld movie cameras, and 1960s fans, the machinist lives in a virtual museum of old-school gadgetry. They'll style a shelving unit with art deco toasters in their loft (appropriately located in an 1910 converted sugar mill) or maintain a driveway full of vintage roadsters. In contrast to collectors who covet precious materials such as crystal, china, and glass, the machinist loves utilitarian objects made of durable finishes like metal that bear signs of heavy use.

Their love of antiquated devices is on one level a rebellion against today's high-tech lifestyle. Many machinists are urban hipsters, the same demographic that listens to vinyl, seeks

---

Scissors are a broad and fascinating world—and thus enticing to collectors. Subtle formal differences are evident between SCISSORS for printmaking and tailoring, shearing sheep and cutting paper goods. This collection includes sewing scissors (the bird-shaped ones), game pieces (the tiniest pair), and numerous desktop models.

fashion inspiration in Grandma's closet, and cooks with heritage pork and heirloom tomatoes. They are less intrigued by cutting-edge technologies than by earlier inventions, harboring a curiosity about the obsolete function of old-school cash registers and hair dryers. Kitting out one's home in tubular-aluminum furniture by Warren McArthur is the machinist's way of celebrating the utopian promise of industrialism while rebelling against the overly fast-paced culture it spawned. This is the collecting equivalent of the slow-foods movement.

Although their passions extend to implements like hammers and cutlery, whose basic form has remained unchanged for millennia, machinists primarily covet industrial-age curios: electric irons, manual typewriters, démodé telephones. To most people, the phrase "factory-made design" conjures images of standardization and sameness. But in fact mass production abetted endless stylistic variety, as did regional differences between local cottage industries. Consider the myriad iterations of cameras, from professional models to Polaroids to bare-bones point-and-shoots. The humble clothes hanger is another household device subject to abundant creative license during the Depression, an era when everyone with get-rich-quick aspirations sought a patent for their proprietary designs, and there was much reinvention of the wheel. (Patent-chasing was the early-twentieth-century equivalent of QVC and infomercials.)

Metal is a common thread to most of these objects, whether machined, stamped, forged, or wrought. Many machinists collect not a product but a material: galvanized steel, cast iron, steel wire. The machinist has an eye for the way finishes patinate, sometimes darkening, other times rusting or blossoming into mottled verdigris. They likewise covet signs of abuse such as dents and dings and scratches. Uninterested in pristine finishes or soft, cuddly forms, they embrace the unprecious side of metal. The ever-practical machinist doesn't want the responsibility of collecting fragile ephemera like majolica, etched crystal, or blown-glass funnels. Objects like hammers and irons can't be broken, which liberates the machinist from worry (mental energy that could be expended on hunting new collectibles).

Indestructibility, coupled with novelty, is at the root of the current trend for repurposing industrial artifacts as interior decoration. Vintage luggage-hauling trolleys and ice carts are the new coffee table, decommissioned baptismal fonts the new garden urn. The vogue for unadorned and unpretentious finishes reflects a broader cultural valuation of authenticity. To the machinist, there's much beauty in how objects age and evolved from use, in the honesty and purity of raw materials. Call it the new machine age.

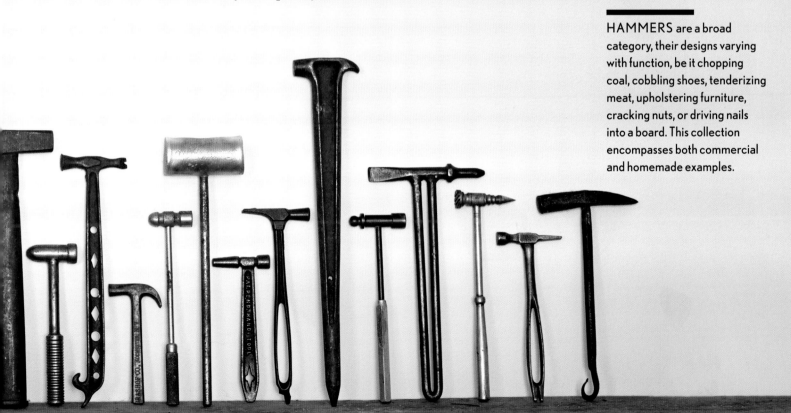

HAMMERS are a broad category, their designs varying with function, be it chopping coal, cobbling shoes, tenderizing meat, upholstering furniture, cracking nuts, or driving nails into a board. This collection encompasses both commercial and homemade examples.

Galvanization was refined in the nineteenth century as a more durable alternative to tinplating sheet metal. The coating provided rustproofing and thus ensured longevity, especially in locations like wharfs and farms where the material was subject to extremes of weather and corrosive forces. GALVANIZED STEEL could be sterilized via spray washing; accordingly, it was utilized for an enormous variety of functional objects, from beverage crates and laundry implements to dustpans.

THIS PAGE A collection of factory-made vintage STOOLS is a testament to the manifold functions of this utilitarian seating category. Some designs were highly engineered, including collapsible, portable models and ones that unfolded to form stepladders for kitchen use or to enter a train. Medical stools were generally enameled for sanitization, while ones for drafting featured a padded leather seat to ensure a comfy workday perch. Milking stools, meanwhile, are quite small in scale and low to the ground.

OPPOSITE Folding TRAVEL HANGERS are often Rube Goldberg–type contraptions, with wacky, jerry-rigged structures that recall medieval torture devices. This was a category that starry-eyed inventors tried to reinvent in search of a patentable (and mass-marketable) design, resulting in endless variety. They often came in sets of three, tucked in a little leather pouch—perfect for overnight train and boat travel.

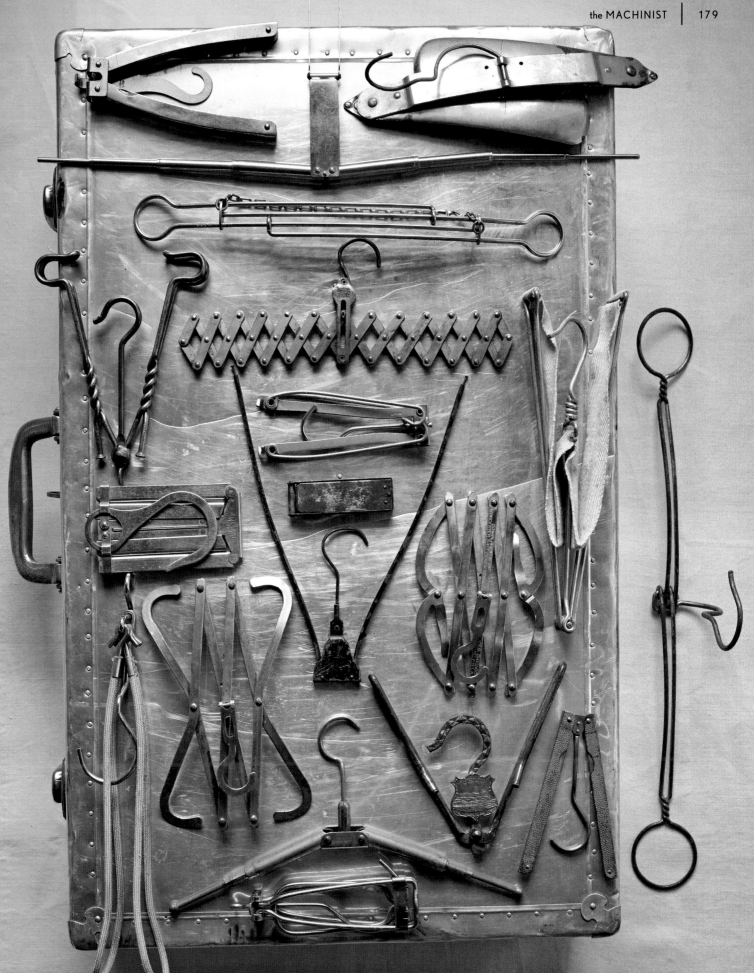

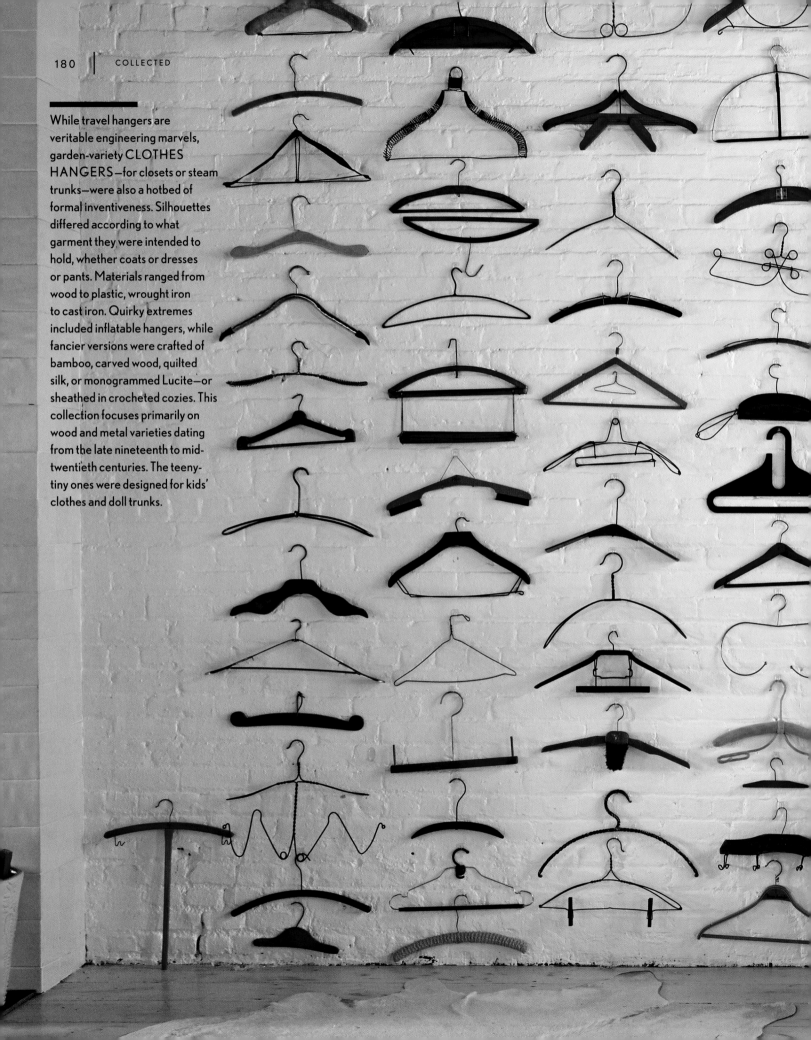

While travel hangers are veritable engineering marvels, garden-variety CLOTHES HANGERS—for closets or steam trunks—were also a hotbed of formal inventiveness. Silhouettes differed according to what garment they were intended to hold, whether coats or dresses or pants. Materials ranged from wood to plastic, wrought iron to cast iron. Quirky extremes included inflatable hangers, while fancier versions were crafted of bamboo, carved wood, quilted silk, or monogrammed Lucite—or sheathed in crocheted cozies. This collection focuses primarily on wood and metal varieties dating from the late nineteenth to mid-twentieth centuries. The teeny-tiny ones were designed for kids' clothes and doll trunks.

The design of utilitarian domestic flatware differed by region depended on vernacular craft techniques and material availability. In farm areas, animal bones were favored, while wood was the norm in verdant locales. There was much variation style, as form followed function: The rivets that hold together the CARBON-STEEL CUTLERY provided an opportunity for makers to bestow a decorative stamp or unique stylistic signature. Some motifs are more common than others; hearts and stars are especially elusive and

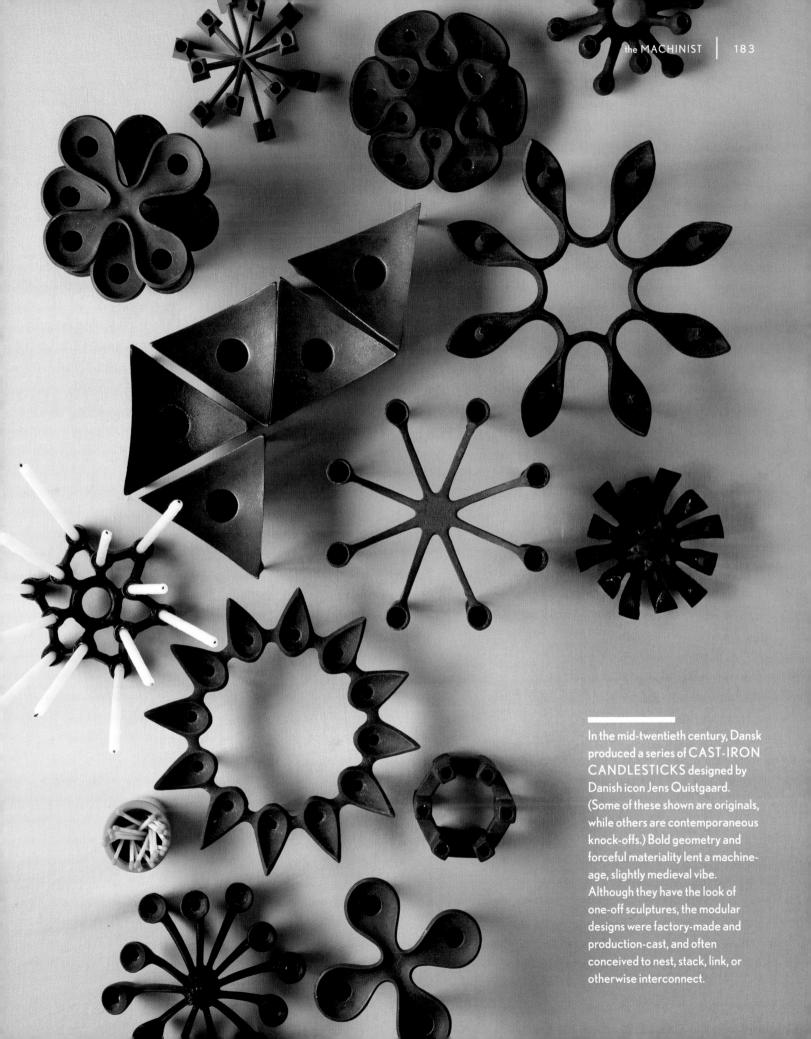

In the mid-twentieth century, Dansk produced a series of CAST-IRON CANDLESTICKS designed by Danish icon Jens Quistgaard. (Some of these shown are originals, while others are contemporaneous knock-offs.) Bold geometry and forceful materiality lent a machine-age, slightly medieval vibe. Although they have the look of one-off sculptures, the modular designs were factory-made and production-cast, and often conceived to nest, stack, link, or otherwise interconnect.

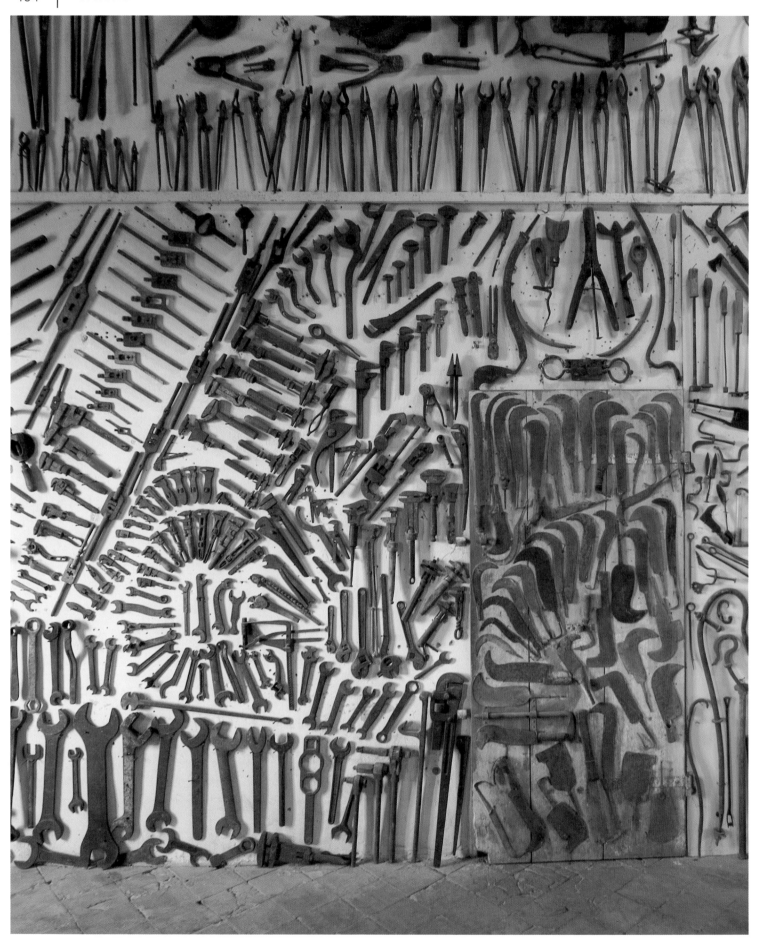

OPPOSITE An entire room in the Museo Guatelli in Parma, Italy, is overtaken by an elaborate installation of handmade WOOD AND METAL TOOLS, from hammers to scissors. The museum, the former residence of collector Ettore Guatelli, is a monument to sixty thousand workaday objects, including clocks, luggage, and even old shoes. The elaborate installation riffs on a practice popular in medieval castles, where weaponry like hatchets, swords, and muskets was displayed in a similarly dynamic, allover fashion—a symbol of the ruler's fortitude.

THIS PAGE What looks like funky line drawings on a wall is actually a collection of vintage RUG BEATERS. All were conceived for the same basic purpose—beating dust out of textiles—but makers took much creative liberty in the sculpting of the metal-wire heads.

Some are quite whimsical, others wholeheartedly utilitarian. Size and shape also varied depending on whether the beater was intended for curtains, pillows, mattresses, or rugs. Most rug beaters were made from metal wire, but wicker and rattan are common, too. You'll often find the long wood handles engraved or stamped with the name of a hardware store; such examples were most likely gifts with purchase when buying a porch mat.

OPPOSITE An architect and his artist wife collect all manner of mid-century creations, including mod 1960s METAL ASHTRAYS by industrial designer Ben Seibel. The sinuous forms, many in brass, betray Seibel's background in sculpture; he also made hard-wearing dishware and other tabletop items.

THIS PAGE The couple designed their home to showcase their many collections, which fill various niches and ledges envisioned for that purpose. An accent wall in a hallway, for instance, was fitted with shelves to form a display vignette for vintage CLOCKS dating from the mid twentieth century, a time when battery-operated and wind-up designs were nascent.

PORTABLE TYPEWRITERS are a precursor to modern-day laptop computers. Much ingenuity informed their design, from the compact forms and collapsing mechanisms to the carrying cases in which they were transported.

Typewriter ribbons were sold in striking TIN CANISTERS bedecked with groovy typographical treatments or pictorial elements. From the 1880s to the 1960s, when the electric typewriter became prevalent, ribbon manufacturers changed tin style every few years. Accordingly, a collection is a veritable mini-dissertation of graphic-design history of the era. Easily scored at flea markets, the small containers—which were always round or square—were often repurposed to store household odds and ends; it's common to find the name of the contents scratched onto the lid.

This machinist lives in a veritable museum of vintage TOASTERS. His holdings, which include everything from American art deco to versions made in communist Germany, were assembled as a sort of microcosm of design history. Machines varied culturally and functionally; some had peculiar bread-turning mechanisms, for instance.

Although his collection includes more than 600 examples, he lives with just 120 on display. The loft-style apartment reiterates the industrial aesthetic of the toasters, which range from constructivist to decorative.

DISPLAYING TOASTERS SIDE BY SIDE
ON LONG SHELVES HIGHLIGHTS THE
UNIQUENESS OF EACH MACHINE.

WOVEN-WIRE BIRD BASKETS, white-glazed fish dishes, ceramic elephant figurines, chicken-themed miscellany—such creatures populate the zoologist's happy menagerie. This collector is hooked on the animal kingdom, buying items related to the species they love. Although the zoologist can be quite specific about what genre they collect, such as dishware, others are less discerning, amassing everything from tapestries to T-shirts in their chosen motif. Accordingly, the zoologist's collection, while unified by a particular breed or species, is often impressively broad in scope. Especially since they have a lot to choose from: Animal imagery is ubiquitous in the decorative-arts and consumer-products worlds, from fauna-inspired majolica to bunny-shaped candy containers, from fine jewelry to corporate logos and sports mascots.

A school of fish swims across a serpentine-tiled wall in a living area; sand-toned fabrics and a giant clamshell augment the beachfront ambience. The FISH-THEMED COLLECTION is quite varied, ranging from a bronze sculpture and ceramic plates to milk-glass figurines and a cast-iron table base.

Don't mistake the zoologist for a naturalist. While the latter loves anything of the earth, the zoologist isn't necessarily a nature buff; they're just obsessed with ponies or poodles. How does the zoologist come to adore a certain animal? One factor is the personality or attitude of a particular beast—a lion's strength, a kitten's cuteness. Or the critter in question is somehow a strong presence in the zoologist's world: A dog lover with a house full of Scotties is bound to collect a few canine statuettes and naïve dog drawings along the way. (There are vintage dealers purveying only Scottie-themed ephemera, so enduringly popular is the motif.)

Often the zoologist personally identifies with the animal collected. A competitive swimmer accumulates a zillion fish tchotchkes; an Aussie expat binges on stuffed kangaroos; an avid birdwatcher wallpapers her den in framed Audubon prints. The animal might be a stand-in for a childhood yearning: A farm-raised urbanite collects chicken kitchenware as a reminder of his youth; the little girl who begged her parents to buy her a horse grows up to overdose on equine bibelots.

Loved ones end up associating the zoologist with this animal, too, and contribute to (or, rather, enable) the collection, giving it a life of its own. In some cases, the collection starts as a joke: A stubborn Taurean is the recipient of stuffed bulls. This is how the zoologist suddenly finds himself living with fifty-five owls, becoming custodian of a world not of his own invention.

Many cultures associate with specific animals. New Zealanders have kiwi birds; the French have honeybees; scarabs have significance to Egyptians, and eagles to Native Americans. Sometimes that creature is a signifier of good fortune or its reverse. Cicadas and ladybugs are tokens of luck in many countries, while a bird in one's home is considered a mischance by the Irish. (Unlucky indeed for the Dublin-dwelling bird buff.)

Animal iconography proliferates in other subcultures, from the zodiac sign to the Chinese calendar. Mythical beasts like the phoenix and thunderbird abound as well: Consider the popularity of unicorn imagery in medieval tapestries. Dolphins and serpents were big in the classical world, and often used for functional objects like andirons and chandelier hooks, perhaps courtesy of their sinuous body shape.

Taxidermy fans fall into the zoologist category, too; think of the game room of a great Adirondack house, presided over by rare and exotic species like giraffe and rhinoceros. But more often, the zoologist is not the sportsman behind the demise of the animals on display. Take the Brooklyn hipster whose studio apartment looks like a Deyrolle outpost: For him, squirrel mounts or stuffed marlins aren't hunting trophies but symbols of beloved creatures whose lives he's honoring via collecting.

Intriguingly, zoologists are often quite restrained in other aspects of their life. They might not even have a collector's disposition to begin with; a love for animals is a primal impulse. But their stockpiling of snakes, frogs, flamingoes, or alligators becomes the one area of their life where they let themselves go, and they do so with wild abandon.

Bottle-stopper fanatics know how rare it is to find these implements garnished with animal shapes. Many were Black Forest souvenirs, their place of origin (Germany or Italy) typically stamped on the bottom. These examples depict the mascots of the Republican and Democratic parties—another widespread zoological motif.

THIS PAGE German toy maker Steiff is best known for handmade mohair teddy bears and high-quality stuffed animals. But in the post-war years, the company unveiled a more affordable line of POM-POM CREATURES targeted to middle-class consumers. Chickadees, sparrows, bunnies, and other cute critters were among the offerings, their pouf-like forms making a sweet impression grouped in a menagerie.

OPPOSITE Aquatic fanatics have ample variety of decorative objects from which to choose, from duck decoys to more obscure categories like JAPANESE FLOWER FROGS. The little vases, typically metal or ceramic, were designed to anchor blossoms in tabletop water gardens (a phenomenon that trended in the 1920s and 1930s). Not just a tool to facilitate the floral arrangement's structure, flower frogs are a decorative element in their own right, their zoomorphic form figuring into the overall composition. And despite their name, the sculptures came in myriad species, including turtles, crocodiles, crabs, carp, and other waterborne creatures.

Some zoologists set their sights on one animal; others—like this crustacean collector—fancy an entire classification of species. Lobsters, shrimps, and crabs had their aesthetic heyday in Victorian times, an era during which crab bisque and lobster thermidor were huge. CRUSTACEAN MOTIFS were common in majolica and other tabletop items like these lobster-topped soup tureens.

Catch-of-the-day collectibles also came in the form of CLAW-SHAPED SALT AND PEPPER SHAKERS.

NESTLE MEAL-TIME ACCOUTREMENTS IN AQUARIUM GRAVEL FOR A CATCHY TWIST ON A SUMMER TABLETOP.

THIS PAGE Pigs are this zoologist's obsession, inspiring the use of porcine wooden CUTTING BOARDS as place settings for a grilled-cheese-and-ham sandwich feast. Each board has a slightly different silhouette, but the common material and format make them feel of a piece.

OPPOSITE Cutting boards are a popular collecting category, and animals a favorite subject; this grouping alone includes a bear, rooster, bunny, mouse, and turtle. One way to tell apart HOMEMADE AND COMMERCIALLY PRODUCED versions: The former are usually made from a single piece of wood.

HUNG ON A WALL OR
PROPPED UP IN BRIGHT-
PAINTED SHELVES, CUTTING
BOARDS BRING A FESTIVE
AND WHIMSICAL TOUCH TO
THE KITCHEN.

Fanciers of feathered friends flock to avian decor, as in this living vignette. Framed PRINTS OF BIRDS—actually eighteenth-century bookplates—are cleverly hung to appear as though they're perching in a forest, an illusion upheld by tree-print wallpaper. Anchoring the seating area is artist Meret Oppenheim's iconic bird-leg table. Courtesy of the refined imagery and muted colors, the tableau feels understated, not overdone.

For ornithology lovers, there's no more coveted collectible than a Havell print by early-nineteenth-century naturalist John James Audubon, author of the seminal *The Birds of America*. This digital reproduction of the artist's snowy owl—a symbol of wisdom—is a more affordable luxury than an original. Taking a cue from the bird's coloration is a collection of AVIAN OBJETS, from bisque porcelain figurines to bone china.

THIS PAGE An enfilade of FISH MOLDS lines an entryway shelf, lending a welcoming touch. Their aged patina mirrors the weatherworn finish of the bench below. Fish platters and sauceboats were common in Scandinavia and other locales where the food is a dietary staple.

OPPOSITE Beginning in the mid-1800s, FISH-SHAPED BOTTLES commonly housed wine, spirits, bitters, and even perfume (note the bottom left bottle, with its finned stopper). The style is easily found in flea markets for affordable prices, although original 1860s specimens are quite desirable and valuable.

The dining room at Bonnet House is embellished with taxidermied FISH MOUNTS, mementos of an avid sportsman's grand life spent yachting and enjoying the outdoors. Quieted by cypress-plank walls, their bold primary hues

Early-nineteenth-century Bacchus mugs—often called SURPRISE MUGS—have a peekaboo effect, submerging an animal that's revealed when the glass is drained. The design derives from an old English pub game, in which (real) frogs and serpents were deviously hidden in the bottom of beer mugs. The mugs are crafted of Pratt-ware ceramic, a warm-bodied soft paste decorated with polychrome.

The world of vintage COOKIE CUTTERS is rife with animal imagery. Housewives would commission their favorite critters from itinerant tinsmiths who traveled from town to town in the nineteenth century. This selection also includes twentieth-century versions, which helped families celebrate all the holidays with animal cookies.

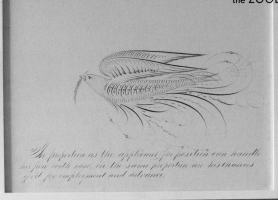

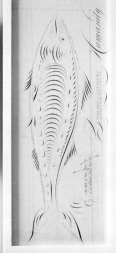

These vintage penmanship drawings were a technique for practicing cursive. Schoolteachers would make students copy elaborate drawings as a way to develop their writing artistry; zoomorphic creatures were a favored subject. ANIMAL PENMANSHIP drawings were a fixture of state fair competitions; the blue ribbon was awarded to whoever could draw the fastest and most artfully. (You'll often find the time written on the back.) This collector gave the disparate drawings a cohesive look with matching all-white frames.

A Scandinavian maker produced these JOINTED TOY MONKEYS in the 1960s. Designed to hang from one another and dangle from the furniture (or even the ceiling), they came in different sizes and styles, from gorillas to baboons.

The FRAMED FOWL look like drawings, but they're actually rendered in feathers, a medium rooted in eighteenth-century England. The pieces hang over a luxurious expanse of early-nineteenth-century toile, its painterly scenes printed via a copper-engraving process. Lovely toiles are still produced by many top textile houses, but nothing approaches the quality and subtlety of traditional copper engraving done by the English and French, each known for its unique imagery— often animal or nature scenes—and color palette.

OPPOSITE This zoologist chickened out, so to speak, with an over-the-top assemblage of fowl. Colorful vintage FARM-THEMED WALLPAPER, framed artworks, and figurines depicting clucking chicks and strutting roosters pair with muslin prints, used as teaching tools at turn-of-the-century 4-H schools.

THIS PAGE Covered dishes used for keeping their contents warm at the table, EGG COZIES came in myriad materials, from crochet to pressed glass. The earliest examples represent nested chickens, but in the Victorian era zoomorphic imagery diversified. In the 1950s, milk-glass chicken dishes become such a phenomenon that collecting clubs reissued vintage designs. Here, a collection that includes cookie jars and egg cups creates a festive centerpiece on a rustic

THIS PAGE Man's best friend makes the perfect welcoming committee, thus the popularity of DOGGIE DOORSTOPS. Often rendered in cast iron, they were made in many breeds and sizes.

OPPOSITE Pets are like family. As a symbol of affection and remembrance, a practice developed of commissioning PORTRAITS of one's cats and dogs. Paintings and photographs are easy to score at vintage shops; naïve homemade versions are especially charming.

THE CONTAINERIST LOVES vessels of all sorts—big or small, humble or high-end, for enclosure or for display. They are connoisseurs of tackle boxes, cheeky trompe l'oeil food tins, metal-mesh egg baskets, glass cheese domes, musical-instrument cases, vintage luggage, and Victorian-era velvet-clad pen packaging. A stack of ribbon-adorned hatboxes or antique aquariums spied at the vintage shop sparks a flurry of ideas about all the ways these containers could be pressed into service, how they could be arranged to make a decorative accent, and what could be showcased or stashed in them.

Containerists are motivated by pragmatism: They love repurposing objects, whether for storage or accessorizing. This collector embraces the ethos of an earlier era when nothing was wasted, and every little scrap of material, no matter how

Even subject to the patina of use and age, vintage TEA CANISTERS still have abundant graphic appeal, with their vibrant colors and Asian-inflected motifs. Spice up an overlooked nook by hanging them on a wall, or cluster them on a counter for decorative punch.

picayune, would be recycled into something else at the end of its lifespan. Giving pretty packaging a new purpose makes the containerist feel whole. In their eyes, salvaged galvanized-steel milk bins are the perfect place to keep toys. Obsolete items like snuff bottles and pap boats can be put to use for floral arrangements and jewelry storage. Rows of espresso cans stacked on the kitchen countertop form a pop-art backsplash while corralling small cooking implements. (An added benefit of containering: Items don't eat up much room in the house since they're generally holding other things.)

One of the most popular vintage collectibles is point-of-sale packaging such as spice containers, tea tins, and Mason jars, many designed specifically for reuse as functional or decorative elements. The Depression sparked the giveaway phenomenon, whereby food makers lured frugal consumers with goods purveyed in containers designed to multitask. Kraft sold dairy items in what were called "swanky swigs," decorative glass jars that doubled as fun freebie juice tumblers once emptied of their original contents. British biscuit company Huntley & Palmers made novelty tins in the guise of engraved-wood tea caddies, Japanese lanterns, and ladies' purses. The high degree of inventiveness and artistry was an early sales tool that enticed customers to buy their brand of products.

In the mid-twentieth century, certain consumer-goods packaging types were also a locus of prominent graphic designers. Icons Paul Rand and Alvin Lustig envisioned containers such as cigar boxes and typewriter-ribbon tins. Such containers are ubiquitous in flea markets and often lovingly careworn, as they were used by a previous generation of crafty containerists to store pushpins, spare buttons, nails, and other odds and ends.

Affordability is a motivator for many containerists. Some of the objects they covet most cost little or no money: quirky bins of indeterminate use, wicker baskets, and recycled packaging are things that everyone of a certain era saved—but that no one perceived as having resale value. A vintage Gucci steamer trunk may be exorbitant, but a no-name aluminum version can be had for a few dollars at the flea market (and is just as effective at storing clothes in your bedroom). Even workaday items like old metal strongboxes and milk bins weren't prized until recently, courtesy of the contemporary vogue for all things industrial chic.

Containerists are motivated by an almost primal urge to keep their material possessions in check (even while furthering their acquisitiveness). Enclosing their clutter in decorative boxes and suitcases helps keep chaos at bay. It lets them be a little crazy on the inside, but neat on the outside. They correlate visual order with mental order; hiding mess allows their mind to rest. Of course, this practical side also allows them to be indulgent; who couldn't use just one more sterling box, perhaps to store the spare change? The very nature of this collecting methodology sparks the imagination, inspiring an infectious creativity that can't be contained.

Aeronautical aluminum, abundant in the post-war era, was utilized to make all manner of household goods, LIGHTWEIGHT SUITCASES among them. Flea market finds can range from early Samsonite and Halliburton to no-name and even homemade versions. Many were designed for travel, but smaller sizes were created to house ice skates, roller skates, and even shirts (this during an era when laundry services necessitated mailing garments in sturdy pressed-tin boxes). Stacked or arrayed in an enfilade style, the vintage luggage doubles as storage.

OPPOSITE British biscuit-maker Huntley & Palmers designed SWEET TINS in the form of inlaid Moroccan side tables, pagodas, phone booths, leather-bound tomes stacked between bookends, and other flights of fancy that were meant to be showcased as decor. Cute idea: Hang the lids on the wall as jewelry pegs (or simply artworks).

THIS PAGE Huntley & Palmers also made tins that mimicked BLUE WEDGWOOD; set in tiers on a console, they're witty stand-ins for the real thing.

OPPOSITE Snuff and tobacco boxes are a seductive lure to containerists. Although the palm-sized accoutrements were often made of luxe materials, these seventeenth- and eighteenth-century DUTCH AND ENGLISH CREATIONS are less precious, probably designed for working-class consumers. The collection includes examples in brass, pewter, and black-lacquered papier-mâché.

THIS PAGE Arranged in groupings of varying heights, the SNUFFBOXES add a vertical element to a tablescape. The containers also make perfect pedestals for other bibelots. For an unexpected accent, display them standing up on one side, splayed open like a book.

OPPOSITE **Convert** antique aquariums into stackable display cases—or simply terrariums—by having plexiglass cut to fit the top. Populating the tanks with collections of colorful vintage FISH FLOATS AND CERAMIC SAND CASTLES of German and Japanese provenance reinforces the under-the-sea mood.

THIS PAGE **Diminutive** early nineteenth-century bottles—most designed to hold SNUFF OR SHOE BLACKING—make ideal vessels for single-bloom floral arrangements. The translucent green and brown hues look lovely on a windowsill, catching light while bringing the coloration of the outdoors in.

Made by itinerant craftsmen in the nineteenth and twentieth centuries, these baskets were designed to carefully TRANSPORT EGGS from henhouse to table without crushing the precious cargo. They were also ideal for kitchen storage; the woven wire kept eggs well aerated. Larger versions were made for potatoes, onions, and other vegetables. The baskets could be submerged in a pot of water to boil their contents.

Designed to cover dairy items and baked goods in kitchens and general stores, BLOWN-GLASS FOOD DOMES protected food from flies and dust—and helped regulate temperature—in the era before window screens and air conditioning were commonplace. Large ones were sized to house a full wheel of cheese, medium ones to cage cakes and pastries, and petite versions to store butter. Use the glass covers for their original purpose or to set off other collectibles.

STRONGBOXES functioned like suitcases, designed to safeguard and transport important documents, money, and even luggage. Sold in sizes ranging from petite to trunk-like, the sturdy boxes were traditionally painted black and detailed with gold stripes to mimic fancy lacquer. When the paint is overly worn, give the containers a new lease on life by stripping and polishing them to expose the underlying tinned steel. Strongboxes retaining their original keys are most coveted since it renders them more functional, allowing them to be lifted by the top handle.

This containerist collects SALVAGED TIN BINS AND MILK CRATES. Tinplated steel ages in painterly mottled patterns as the outer skin wears off to expose the underlying raw steel; displayed side by side, they look like a Giorgio Morandi still life.

HERMÈS
PARIS

Erwan

Ms. Piper Williams

OPPOSITE Vintage packaging from luxury brands like Tiffany's and Cartier, known for their signature hues, are often recycled as fun (and attractive) containers. A pyramidal stack of bright-orange HERMÈS BOXES doubles as organizing device and ornamental display.

THIS PAGE A grouping of antique Chinese BRUSH POTS clusters on a wall-hung console. Their forms are sublimely spare, attenuated cylinders or cones sculpted of natural materials like a hollowed-out tree branch or carefully selected bamboo slice. This collection boasts a range of sizes, functions, and materials, from Japanese lacquer to precious stone.

Used to feed gruel to the infirm,
these eighteenth-century SILVER
PAP BOATS are like shallow
gravy boats but with wider spouts.
The collector covets their archaic
purpose and sinuous proto-
modernist forms.

Victorian-era staples, VELVET-COVERED BOXES were used to merchandise and package jewelry, silverware, sheet music, and ladies' dresser-top items, such as shoe-button hooks, glove stretchers, and cuticle scissors. Sometimes sculpted or stamped with patterns like flocked wallpaper, the fabric wears into a gorgeously threadbare surface. The boxes were keepers: Even the hardware was elegantly designed.

EXPLOIT AN UNDERUTILIZED OTTOMAN OR SIDE TABLE FOR A DISPLAY AREA: USE BOTH THE TOP SURFACE AND THE FLOOR SPACE BELOW TO CREATE A LANDSCAPE-LIKE TABLEAU, GROUPING ITEMS BY COLOR.

THIS PAGE A collection of late nineteenth-/early-twentieth-century Sterling silver boxes are stashed in a Lucite shelving system, below a vignette of white CHINOISERIE CERAMIC OBJETS. The boxes mirror the room's mod decor and silver and white palette.

OPPOSITE STERLING BOXES hail from all over the world but are primarily Mexican-made. Each features a different technique, from repoussé to dimensional hammering. These were probably made as souvenirs, hence the slightly kitschy Aztec and Mayan motifs; Mexico City and Guadalajara were particularly popular American tourist destinations starting in the 1900s.

THE ARTIFICIALIST COULD, at first glance, be mistaken for a nature buff, which is not so far from the truth. This collector's world abounds with leaves, fruits, fluttering insects, and trees of life. But natural materials are not the draw; it's natural *imagery*—flora and fauna filtered through an artistic lens and translated into another medium. They love nature in a more durable and permanent form, surrounding themselves with luscious-looking things that defy decay. The artificialist flocks to brass leaves, carved-stone fruits, faux-malachite wallpaper, and enameled-metal butterfly pins. Like all collectors, they are lured by a subconscious pull to certain objects and iconography, but there's an extra layer to their affection: a fascination with how artisans and craftspeople interpret the world around them.

Faux fleurs are an obsession of many an artificialist (as well as those with a black thumb.) This collector, an artist who loves bright colors and sparkly finishes, enjoys springtime year-round via her collection of BEADED BLOOMS. It's like the persistence of memory, conjuring up spring whenever she wants it. She arranges them as she would real flowers, placing them in a vase and blending individual stems.

Artificialists fall into two extremes: those who fetishize verisimilitude, and those who appreciate a more self-conscious brand of artifice. The former covets lifelike depictions—antique botanical paintings, faux bonsai that pass for real. The latter prowls flea markets in search of crocheted vegetables and flowers made from sliced-up tin cans. The two types have opposing attitudes

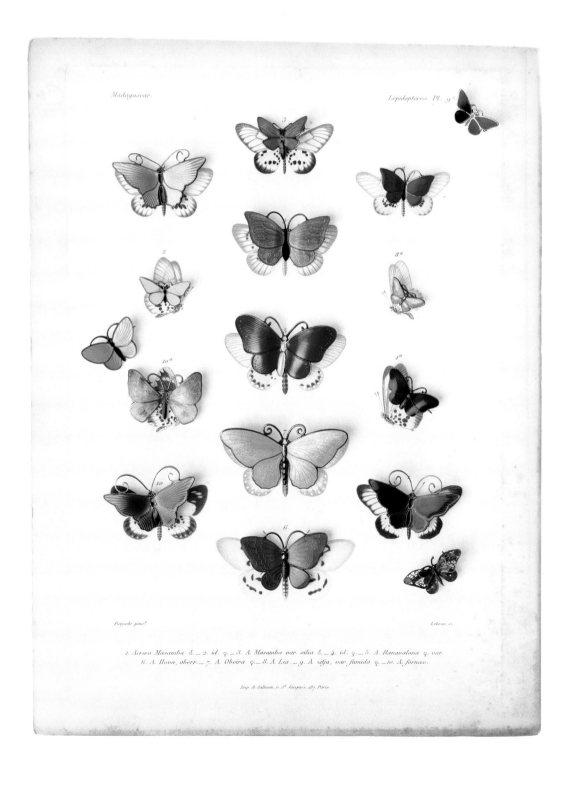

and sensibilities. The literalist is awed by the artistry and technical facility that underlies mimicry, while the ironist appreciates the wink-wink humor inherent in less faithful, more stylized representations. It's the difference between loving Pierre-Joseph Redouté's naturalistic depiction of hibiscus blooms and pop artist Andy Warhol's screen-print version.

Nature is not the sole motivation of this collector. Many artificialists love trompe l'oeil in general: framed needlepoints that, from across the room, look like painted canvases; a rolled-up magazine, tucked under a lady's arm, that's actually a chic clutch. This collector loves things that are trying hard to deceive. Artificialists revel in optical illusions and double takes, the surprise of discovery that an object or material is not what it seems.

Artificialism has a storied history. In Western fine art, the tyranny of literalism didn't lift until the late-nineteenth-century advent of modernism; prior to that, style was largely driven by refinement of technique and draftsmanship in pursuit of lifelike depictions of the world. Farther east, eighteenth-century Chinese scholarly objects imitated natural materials like leaves, wood, and stones in porcelain. And in the decorative arts arena, myriad materials were developed to mimic more precious varieties. Consider Sheffield plate and silver lusterware, which simulate sterling, and gold leaf, developed to look like solid gold.

Venerable handicrafts like beaded flowers are another staple of the artificialist's decor. The glittery bouquets have their origin in sixteenth-century Venice, when local ladies were enlisted to craft the faux *fiores* to adorn churches; the intricate beadwork was resurgent in Victorian times and in the post–World War II era as faddish pastimes of the leisure class and homemakers. The artificialist is drawn to such examples of human dexterity and repetitive achievement—the notion of busy hands. They value the human touch *and* the human mind, the places where craftsmanship and intellect collide.

Butterflies are a common JEWELRY MOTIF, especially rendered in enamel. Certain colors and combinations are rarer than others; blue is common while pink is more obscure. Some of the most beautiful examples were executed by mid-century Scandinavian designers such as David Andersen, who sparked a global craze for bold enameling.

OPPOSITE **Teeny-tiny beads were employed by amateur and professional artisans to create faux renditions of plant life as well as related imagery, like baskets. The craft of making BEADED FLOWERS started in European churches as a less expensive (and all-season) alternative to decorating the altar with fresh flowers. The genre became popular again in the 1950s with the mass marketing of bead kits to hobbyists.**

THIS PAGE **Often made by crafty amateurs, petals sculpted from (and stored in) RECYCLED CANS have abundant personality. Cutting blooms from food cans was an especially sweet (and common) way to celebrate ten years of marriage—the tin anniversary.**

Bug jewelry spans the centuries, from ancient Egyptian scarab rings to bee-themed earrings in eighteenth-century France. Many species are abuzz with cultural significance or symbolic value as well: The cicada, for instance, is a sign of good luck. The category is quite broad, making it an easy entry point for neophyte collectors: In addition to brooches, there are hat pins, combs, earrings, necklaces, and more, in materials ranging from gold and silver to Lucite and Bakelite.

This artificialist's obsession with bug jewelry is rooted in her love of nature. Her collection of INSECT-MOTIF BROOCHES AND PINS includes about two hundred pieces, some lifelike, others quite stylized.

An assortment of BEJEWELED DRAGONFLIES alights on a cluster of (real) long-lasting chrysanthamuns. Consider storing jewelry in a manner that lets it double as display; you can even array pieces in specimen boxes.

OPPOSITE **Bring stylized nature into your home via antique BOTANICAL PRINTS like these** hand-colored fruit engravings. This collector displays her framed pears and apples alongside same-themed figurines in a desk vignette, offset by wallpaper in a similarly tart hue.

THIS PAGE **These Italian marble GRAPE CLUSTERS are** incredibly lifelike—an illusion enhanced by displaying them in a giant planter with the feel of a fruit bowl. The collectibles are incredible pieces of workmanship: Each grape is hand-drilled and braided onto a metal "vine." Even the loveliest bunch of grapes will eventually shrivel into raisins, but these beauties will never spoil.

Ersatz trees make whimsical decorative accents, whether freestanding or designed to hang on a wall. Collectors have abundant styles to choose from, including TOPIARIES, BONSAIS, AND GOLDEN RAIN TREES. Many prime examples are Grand Tour or early Victorian, but they were made all over the world. These examples include versions in shell, wire, and glass.

Kitschy FAKE FRUITS made of cheap, colored plastic give the genre a bad rap, but there exist tasteful vintage versions made of blown glass, beads, carved wood, or precious stone like alabaster. These artful faux grapes and pears are rendered in stone, so they're always fresh—a perfect marriage of practicality and whimsy. Handcrafted by Chinese artisans, they sport leaves made of jade or carnelian, affixed via silk stems.

THIS PAGE Italian-made novelty MAGAZINE CLUTCHES were a big trend in the 1970s. What looks like a folded-up magazine when tucked under the arm of a girl about town is actually just a sheet of paper—printed with the cover of a fashion or shelter magazine—slipped inside a snap-open Perspex or Lucite case. Love for this cheeky design was revived when *Sex and the City's* Carrie Bradshaw sported one in the series' famous Staten Island Ferry scene.

OPPOSITE One of the wittier examples of artificialism: CROCHETED FOODSTUFFS, like this cake, hot dog, and ice-cream sundae. They're so cheeky in their fakeness, this collector covets them like pieces of pop art; the Budweiser wallpaper reinforces the zaniness.

Homemade FAMILY TREES are an inspired twist on collecting antique nature prints. They were widespread in the nineteenth century, spurred by a growing interest in genealogy. The templates were typically lithographs or hand-drawn trees—generally giant oaks—with lines for filling in relatives' names. (The top one was made by an ambitious crafter using cat whiskers.)

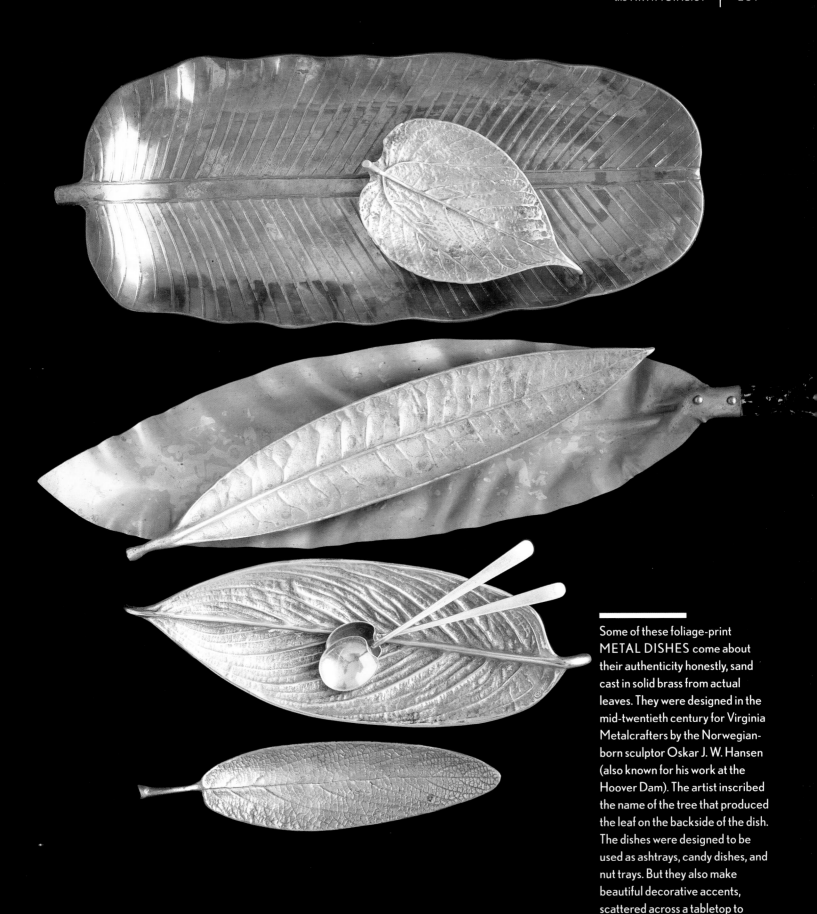

Some of these foliage-print
METAL DISHES come about
their authenticity honestly, sand
cast in solid brass from actual
leaves. They were designed in the
mid-twentieth century for Virginia
Metalcrafters by the Norwegian-
born sculptor Oskar J. W. Hansen
(also known for his work at the
Hoover Dam). The artist inscribed
the name of the tree that produced
the leaf on the backside of the dish.
The dishes were designed to be
used as ashtrays, candy dishes, and
nut trays. But they also make
beautiful decorative accents,
scattered across a tabletop to
conjure an autumnal feeling

THIS PAGE This artificialist collects vintage needlepoint based on iconic works of modern art; his holdings include BLUE-CHIP "PAINTINGS" of pieces by Andy Warhol, Henri Matisse, Peter Max, and Jean Miró. Framed and mounted salon-style on the wall, they're a whimsical nod to the real thing.

OPPOSITE A closeup of a cubist "canvas" reveals the pixelated stitch work. Institutions like Winterthur and The Metropolitan Museum of Art still sell NEEDLEPOINT KITS based on renowned masterpieces in their collection, but the trompe l'oeil tradition dates back to the mid-century, when the kits were first marketed to crafters and hobbyists.

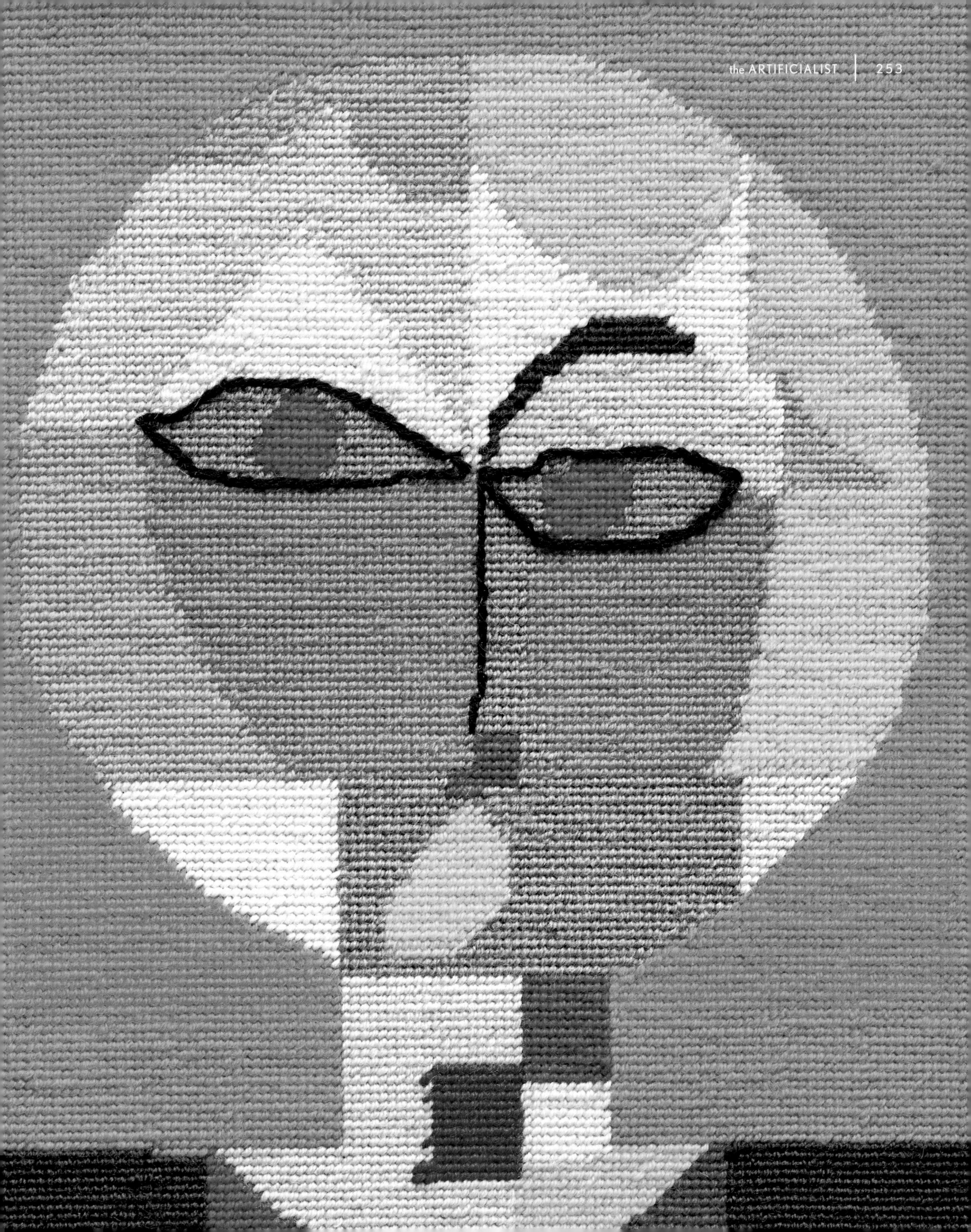

THE COLLECTOR'S NATURAL HABITAT is typically the flea market or vintage shop. Not so the naturalist, for whom the great outdoors is ground zero. They prefer scoring finds at the water's edge and in the forest, with the sun on their cheeks, the wind at their backs, and luck on their side. There the naturalist forages for fossils, arrowheads, and feathers. The beach is especially fertile ground for scavenging weatherworn driftwood, starfish, and sea glass lovingly smoothed over by the sands of time. (True fact: Otherwise rational people go *insane* for sea glass.) The naturalist is deeply engaged with Mother Earth; the living world is their lifeblood.

Collecting FEATHERS during coastal strolls sparked this beachcomber's feature wall: She tapes up her specimen into an ad hoc, and ever-growing, installation. The architecture also bears a naturalist's touch: The owner stripped back a generic 1970s bungalow to its underlying, raw construction for a more elemental quality. Even the table and chairs exhibit a WEATHERWORN PATINA and earth-toned palette.

Compared to other collectors, the naturalist traffics in accessible (if hard-earned) fare, free and ubiquitous items that might even be native to their own backyard—palm fronds, tree branches, dried leaves, and heirloom gourds, to name a few. But, as for all serious collectors, the commonplace or even the slightly unusual won't do. They apply a discerning eye to their favored genre, choosing a scarcer subset that transports the everyday to the exotic: heart-shaped rocks, exuberantly spotted Petoskey-stone fossils. (Geology, of course, holds a strong appeal.) The thrill of the hunt and the rarity of certain naturally occurring features is a major lure.

Naturalists generally prefer collectibles in their raw state, such as rough-hewn chunks of unpolished crystal or sand dollars plucked right off the beach. But some favor a bit more refinement, seeking out objects made from organic materials. Consider carved-burl-wood treen, iridescent wampum beads, malachite decoy eggs, Victorian keepsake boxes mosaicked in seeds or dried beans, or a glittery geode transformed into a lamp base—functional (and decorative) objects that still celebrate the naturalism of the finish. Animal-based finishes like horn, hooves, tortoiseshell, fur, hair, and shells fall into this category, too. The naturalist champions purity of material, even if that material has been given an artful twist or honed to a brilliant but variegated sheen.

Many types of collectors have a taste for "living" materials like leather and metal that develop a patina as they age. But the naturalist values things that are quite *literally* living. They often take a keen (at times scholarly) interest in botany and horticulture, collecting plants and seeds, lichen and seaweed. They might maintain a greenhouse lush with orchids or bonsai, play guardian to a grove of citrus or camelia bushes handed down through the generations, or simply attend to an overabundance of houseplants. In some cases, they may not even collect an object per se, but an experience. Case in point: a bird watcher who maintains a journal of their sightings. Naturalists also honor the full cycle of birth, growth, and rebirth, even celebrating evidence of decay like speckled mold blossoming on picked-a-few-weeks-ago gourds.

As much as naturalists appreciate objects in their unadulterated state, they also love to put their own stamp on their collection—taming the wild, so to speak. They can be quite inventive about showing off their wares. Rather than keep their sand dollars stored in a box under the bed, they'll corral them in a velvet-lined jewelry box. And they'll find vessels that allow their manzanita branches to recline just so, extending an elegant arm like a shy gentleman inviting a lady to dance. Coral and quartz are placed on pedestals, under display domes, or in specimen jars and boxes. Craftier naturalists might array their stones in a spiral on the coffee table, or frame oversized pressed leaves to create graphic wall decorations.

As an extension of their love of flora and fauna, the naturalist often amasses related accoutrements like terrariums, planters, fish tanks, and birdcages. Collectibles in their own right, they are typically put to work as display vignettes—to showcase other prized possessions, naturally.

A gathering of ROTUND GOURDS showcases the fruit's quirky personality. As the gourds dry, painterly mold patterns begin to materialize, revealing the beauty inherent to decay. With their voluptuous forms, gourds look beautiful styled in a plainspoken tableau on a dining table or console.

Seashells are an especially popular canvas for artistry and object of collector lust. Flea-market habitués can find them engraved into cameos, fashioned into demitasse spoons, applied liberally to sailors' valentines, and sliced thin into mother-of-pearl for inlaying accessories.

THIS PAGE **SAILORS' VALENTINES** are small boxes or obelisks covered with a kaleidoscopic mosaic of tiny shells. As the name suggests, mariners returning from sea brought home these tokens of affection for loved ones. Some were crafted by the sailors themselves, whiling away downtime on the ship. The more refined vintage versions found at flea markets and antiques shops were made by artisans and sold at waterfront souvenir shops.

OPPOSITE A tony vanity area has the feel of a **GROTTO**, courtesy of walls and ceiling dressed entirely in seashells, arranged in a manner to mimic wainscoting and architectural paneling. Although the execution is grand, the idea is stunningly simple: The shells are embedded into cement-skimmed walls—a treatment ideal for showers or patio pavers, too. The mirror is likewise clad with shells, revealing the naturalist's strong impulse to encrust.

THIS PAGE By her teens, a young beachcomber had amassed an enviable and impeccable collection of pristine SAND DOLLARS in every size and condition. She houses her bounty in a vintage jewelry box, sorted by size (and accompanied by a handful of seahorses and starfish).

OPPOSITE Artist Frederic Clay Bartlett designed this magical pavilion to showcase wife Evelyn's collection of SHELL AND CORAL. (The round aerie is in the couple's property, Bonnet House, now operated as a museum.) Bartlett even used shells to create crown molding and to outline the recessed display shelving, painted acid yellow so the white shells pop.

THIS PAGE A vignette of posh SHELL AND MOTHER-OF-PEARL objects accents a vanity, lending unpretentious elegance. Natural materials like horn, tortoise, and seashell take on a more cultivated look when polished to a smooth luster and used to embellish all forms of decorative boxes, cases, and the like—from compacts to opera glasses.

OPPOSITE At the north loggia of Bonnet House, Bartlett traced a doorway in a border of shells, culminating in a mosaic frieze of a soaring eagle.

OPPOSITE Courtesy of their scoop shape, shells were used as spoons by the ancients. Millennia later, they're still repurposed for the same function. Victorian-era SOUVENIR SPOONS, sold to tourists at seaside towns, are symbols of Grand Tour exoticism. They were typically marked with the name of the resort or town—either in the bowl or on the handle. Often fashioned from abalone and mollusk shells, some designs are quite fine, others charmingly coarse and crude.

THIS PAGE Dating from the late 1800s, this FAUX-BOIS AQUARIUM—actually crafted of terra-cotta—has a rusticated quality. Aquarium and terrarium arranging were popular Victorian pastimes.

OPPOSITE Bonnet House is also renowned for its greenhouse, which showcases Evelyn Bartlett's ORCHIDS. During her lifetime, the property played host to some 1,000 plants—one of the largest collections in the United States. The naturalist theme carries through to the floor, paved in native CORAL STONE. Here, the same bold yellow paint used elsewhere holds its own with the colorful blooms.

THIS PAGE A medieval invention, BEE SKEPS were made by coiling bound skeins of straw. Vintage versions are a hot commodity, popularized by the modern revival of beekeeping—especially in urban areas. Although no longer used by professional beekeepers (they're actually illegal for farming applications), these basket-like relics of a bygone era convey the air of a nineteenth-century French apiary.

OPPOSITE **Two naturalist obsessions—eggs and exotic geology—collide in these ORNAMENTAL OVA.** A naturalist created an apropos pedestal for her collection by tucking them in little nests. These examples display a diversity of materials (exotic stones, wood, metal, brass) and forms (Russian nesting eggs, pillboxes, decoys used to coax hens to lay). Many are sewing-related, from sock-darning orbs to measuring tapes.

THIS PAGE **Every fall, this family saves the STEMS from their Halloween pumpkins, a timeline of holidays past.** They can be quite lyrical and elegant when dried, with curlicue tendrils and a variegated ombré patina.

THE BOXY GEOMETRY OF
THE FRAMES CREATES A
NICE COUNTERPART TO THE
LEAVES' ORGANIC SHAPES.

OPPOSITE Above a desk, a bouquet of framed, pressed CECROPIA LEAVES makes an eye-catching statement. The oversized leaves were carefully cut and tiled together, so the motif extends from piece to piece.

THIS PAGE Heirloom-seed enthusiasts aren't just collecting a species; they're memorializing (and romanticizing) an earlier, unpolluted era. Although the heirloom-seed movement has grown exponentially in recent years, this naturalist was way ahead of the curve, having collected PUMPKINS, SQUASH, GOURDS, and other unhybridized indigenous plants for almost two decades. Displaying the fruits of her harvest alongside shapely glass bottles highlights the similarity between forms.

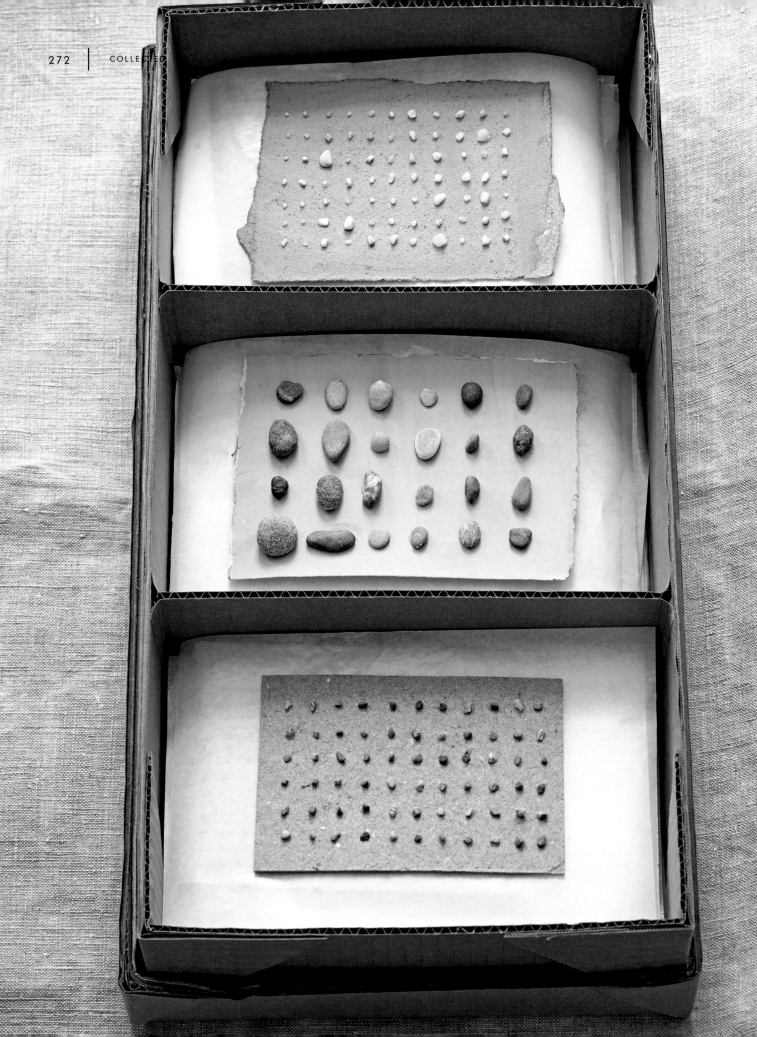

OPPOSITE **Prosaic stones are reborn as fine art when mounted on a pretty backdrop in a graphic pattern. This collection was borne of a family trip to Paros, Greece. Unable to pack their favorite beach and take it home with them, they did the next best thing: lug back a bag of PEBBLES in their suitcase. Once at home, the rocks were sorted by size and color and glued to paper, spaced according to the mood of the day—a sort of daily meditation on a summer week near the sea.**

THIS PAGE **The modernist architect Walter Gropius shared a desk with his wife and collaborator, Ise, at their house in Lincoln, Massachusetts. The work surface (designed by fellow Bauhausian Marcel Breuer) is like a scrapbook of the couple's travels and daily life, populated with STONES, BRANCHES, AND OTHER EPHEMERA collected from walks. The walnut desk sat below a north-facing ribbon window that framed the surrounding landscape, so the couple could work immersed in nature.**

OPPOSITE The Vizcaya Museum and Gardens in Miami embodies the naturalist's love of horticulture. The Italianate villa was the winter residence of industrialist James Deering, who collaborated with landscape architect Diego Suarez and art director Paul Chalfin to curate a spectacular gardenscape dotted with ORCHIDS, SUBTROPICAL PLANTS, AND ANCIENT LIVE OAKS—many relocated from other sites.

THIS PAGE Deering also collected antique statuary, coral stone, and European ARCHITECTURAL FRAGMENTS, including a fifteenth-century outdoor fountain from Italy. The pylons lining the grotto's reflecting pool were carved on site.

OPPOSITE Native fossiling is an abiding fixation of the naturalist, who falls for dessert roses, Cape May Diamonds, Petoskey stones, quartz, and pyrite in their raw form. Such a collection is like the history of the world: MINERALS are the most ancient thing to collect, a symbol of the earth's core and origin. It's a thousand years of pressure and evolution, all in one little object in your house.

THIS PAGE This collector, a photographer, saves a HANDFUL OF SAND from every beach he visits. He stores the sand in small glass spice jars, labeled by location—an easily replicable idea that hardly costs anything yet is a wonderfully transporting memento. The collection is displayed along a shelf in the living room, giving it a place of prominence among artworks.

FOR MOST ENTHUSIASTS, COLLECTING is a nonstop, all-encompassing, 24/7 endeavor. They live and breathe their passion on a daily basis, integrating mid-century West German pottery or wild-west landscapes into their everyday décor. The seasonalist, in contrast, concentrates their collecting efforts on a single occasion, be it a holiday (Christmas), a time of year (fall), or a sporting event (the America's Cup). They may collect stuffed reindeers, flag pins, or yacht-themed objects year-round, but the collection itself only gets paraded out once a year, often for just a handful of days. Three dozen ceramic turkey tureens flock to the dining table for Thanksgiving and then retreat into deep storage after the festivities conclude.

The seasonalist is a pragmatist at heart for whom overabundance is anathema. Christmas is often the exception, a time when they feel emboldened to go all out and ornament not only their tree but also their home (and even their car and front yard)—knowing it's a temporary indulgence. Many will forgo traditionalism and choose unexpected elements such as the vintage PLASTIC TREE that sparked this icy tableau.

What makes this collector especially fascinating isn't the curatorial methodology or the decision-making process behind selecting this particular snowman or hula-girl bobber versus that one. It's when and how they choose to showcase their treasures: in a full-on, over-the-top manner—but for a limited viewing. Seasonalists are typically rational, sensible individuals with a disciplined approach to homemaking and decoration. They're forever seeking

out ways to simplify their environment and streamline its maintenance, and collecting runs counter to that impulse. So they develop a fetish that periodically comes out of the closet—literally and figuratively. A collector who inhabits a tasteful earth-toned abode festoons every surface with hundreds of rabbit-shaped plastic candy containers every Easter. A buttoned-up banker showcases his equine bibelots only during the Kentucky Derby.

The opposing urges—self-control and self-indulgence—are symbiotic and mutually enabling. The seasonalist can live an otherwise practical existence because they have a joyous outlet for their fantasy and thrive on the anticipation of its reveal. Their collection is the one area of their life where they let themselves go completely wild. In this way, the seasonalist—like all collectors—is just exercising a unique brand of restraint. The appetite for acquisition and display is there but totally compartmentalized and controlled. Except for December, when the vintage German snow babies take over. (An extreme version of the seasonalist dedicates a whole room of their house to their obsession.)

Holidays, unsurprisingly, are a major motivator for seasonalists. Christmas holds a particularly strong pull (even among the nondenominational), offering an excuse to amass Czech beaded ornaments, glass kugels, deer figurines, snow globes, feather trees, cardboard villages, and nutcrackers. Judaica is another big category, especially since so little survived the eighteenth and nineteenth centuries. Really, every religious and cultural holiday presents a collecting opportunity: Chinese New Year, St. Patrick's Day, Passover, Diá de los Muertos, Bastille Day, Mardi Gras, Kwanzaa. Particularly in the last two decades, Halloween has become a phenomenon, with obsessives spending untold sums on vintage cardboard ornaments and jack-o'-lantern candy containers. And old-fashioned holidays like Arbor Day, Flag Day, and May Day, which have a diminished role today, were once occasions when people bought all manner of party favors and tabletop accessories—now coveted by today's antique hunters.

But holidays aren't the sole purview of the seasonalist. Sports events are another arena of enticement, fair game for collecting everything from autographed baseballs and Olympic pins to numbered jerseys and vintage trophies. And the arrival of winter, spring, summer, or fall is all the excuse some people need to pull out the vintage watering can collection or harvest-themed table settings. Seasonalism is the one collecting style motivated by weather change, and the impulse is deep-rooted: Many holidays—whether religious or commercial—were conceived to celebrate the new beginning of spring and the abundance of the fall harvest.

Ultimately, the particular season collected is really just a stand-in, a symbol with deeper connotations—whether romance, community, patriotism, or family togetherness. A defining moment of childhood is the frequent cause: Their whole adult life is about maintaining the magical glee of Christmas morning. They can never get past the memory. And why should they, with such a tantalizing trove of collectibles to recapture it for them once a year?

A popular collectible, vintage SNOWMEN are commonplace in flea markets across the globe. You'll typically find them made of blown glass, plastic, or—conjuring the soft feel of freshly fallen snow—pressed cotton. With their small scale, sweet personality, and quiet colorways, these holiday decorations avoid being too cloying.

Christmas trees need not look Christmasy. The off-kilter charm of an aerodynamic BONSAI—accented with deers—is perfect for a tabletop.

LEFT Mid-century Finnish designer Tapio Wirkkala's iconic AVENA VASES look like they were sculpted from blocks of ice. Chic and timeless, the glass vessels are truly all-seasonal. But they take on a more wintry character when filled with berry branches.

BOTTOM LEFT Another way to collect seasonally is by color: green for Christmas, for instance. This tree is potted in a mid-century ceramic in a VERDANT GLAZE popularized by Wedgwood and copied ad nauseam. Add matching balls, and voilà: a modern and monochromatic tabletop.

BOTTOM RIGHT Nodding to Dasher and Prancer, a collection of nineteenth-century DEER FIGURINES cast in lead and bronze cozy up to a Christmas tree adorned with glittery glass icicles. Among them are prized Vienna bronzes, a genre of Austrian-made sculpture coveted for its naturalism. (They were made by the same factory that produced toy soldiers.) The deer came in all sizes and poses, from frolicking to sitting, but the white-painted snow-deer versions are more obscure.

This sartorially minded seasonalist celebrates the advent of winter by pulling out his collection of wool TAM-O'-SHANTERS. The pom-pommed hats are Scottish in origin; authentic versions feature the label of the family clan inside the brim. Tam-o'-shanters aren't the only toppers to symbolize a season: Easter bonnets signaled the arrival of spring.

Seasonally switching out one's wardrobe of home textiles is an old-fashioned ritual still practiced today. Instead of relegating linens, hand towels, and tablecloths to the cupboard and the occasional family meal, consider stitching them into festive curtains or cushions. The pillows here are made from CHRISTMAS HANKIES, a genre distinguished by nearly endless variety.

OPPOSITE Vintage handkerchiefs and LINENS form a collecting category akin to postcards and candy containers: Eagle-eyed collectors can find one to represent practically every holiday. Be strategic and transform them into décor, stretching or framing them like fine artwork.

THIS PAGE Christmas-loving seasonalists adore placing a tree in every room—each decorated in a different theme. A merry alternative to a traditional fir: an artificial version with branches made of feathers. This one channels a mountain village when adorned with vintage CARDBOARD GINGERBREAD HOUSES. Finding them in pristine shape is uncommon, as cardboard is relatively fragile and the cellophane windows and doors rarely intact.

Valentine's Day is for lovers—of heart-shaped trinkets, that is. HEART LOCKETS AND CHARMS make wonderful adornments for wrists, ears, and necks, but don't forget vanities and tabletops, too. Although it became a commercial phenomenon in the early twentieth century, providing ample opportunities for seasonalists (and consumers) to flex their collecting muscles, the holiday is actually rooted in ancient Rome. This array includes charms in some of the most common materials: geology, early plastics, glass, gold, and silver.

OPPOSITE **Stalking imagery of favorite statesmen has long been a faddish pastime, and the calendar's multiple patriotic holidays invite seasonalists to bring these collectibles to center stage. Especially ubiquitous is GEORGE WASHINGTON– THEMED MEMORABILIA,** which range from commemorative coins and bookends to piggy banks and vintage souvenir spoons. An assortment of the latter includes ones bearing the president's profile as well as whimsical depictions of axes, cherry trees, and buildings named after him.

THIS PAGE **Novelty CANDY CONTAINERS cover all the seasons—from New Year's to Christmas. Rabbits, of course, are the signature for Easter;** German-made containers from the late nineteenth century are the most wonderfully (and outrageously) designed. Can you discern the real rabbit from the decoys, made of hand-painted plaster and papier-mâché?

THIS PAGE Stars and stripes (and sparkly rhinestones) forever: The market for patriotic flag imagery is huge and ever growing, but a bejeweled pin can still be had for five dollars at the flea market, if you're lucky. These twinkly RHINESTONE FLAG PINS span the full stylistic spectrum; included are ones from the early twentieth century, when the genre first became popular.

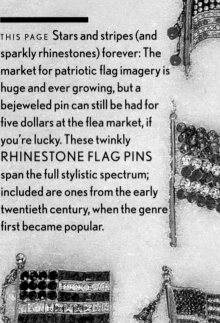

OPPOSITE Every country has its celebratory season of patriotism, and for France it's July 14—Bastille Day. One collector trots out her RED, WHITE, AND BLUE DISHWARE and flag-inspired accents to pay tribute to the birthday of the French republic. Some seasonalists use their living room as their canvas, others their front porch; but for many, the dining room table is ground zero.

THIS PAGE The iridescent tint of vintage CARNIVAL GLASS suits it to fall feasts. Use this shimmery dishware for an autumnal meal or an upscale Halloween cocktail party. Rotating table settings were practically de rigueur in the days before the invention of the automatic dishwasher; hand washing dishes three meals a day makes one crave variety. The glassware's heyday was the century between 1870 and 1970.

OPPOSITE Used seasonally, the pressed glassware reads less whimsical, more elegant. Carnival glass gets its sheen from a metallic spray coating. Its PEACHY TINT fairly glints when set against a grounding backdrop of earthy charcoal.

There's nothing wrong with a potted Norfolk Island pine bedecked with miniature balls to symbolize Christmas, but why not think outside the box? Below a wall-mounted wooden DEER'S HEAD—a cheeky take on taxidermy—is a gathering of vintage fauna in celluloid.

In contrast to many seasonalist obsessions, BACCHUS JUGS (and most Halloween items) are decidedly not cutesy. Quite the opposite—they're a bit scary and weird. Bacchus was the Roman god of the harvest, and his likeness was used to symbolize a time of abundance.

A CHEERLEADER STACK IS A FUN WAY TO DISPLAY ANY TYPE OF MUG—SEASONAL OR NOT.

THIS PAGE You can't celebrate Thanksgiving without TURKEY TCHOTCHKES. A perfect centerpiece: vintage candy containers, such as these strutting fowl in handpainted paper composition. These examples are unusually large in scale and—most uncommon—include a rare female version.

OPPOSITE This collector lives in Michigan, where winters seem never-ending; for her, Thanksgiving is a long season. So she keeps her collection of TURKEY PLATES on display year-round. She is a more extreme version of seasonalist, for whom a once-temporary collection evolves into an entire room; the plates' color palette inspired the surrounding decor. Most of her plates date from the early twentieth century, including one by art deco British ceramicist Clarice Cliff (bottom left).

WINTER IS THE IDEAL TIME TO INDULGE IN SEASONALISM, SINCE MANY OF US ARE MAROONED INSIDE, THE DAYS ARE SHORT, AND WE SEEK OUT WAYS TO BRIGHTEN OUR HOMES AND LIFT OUR SPIRITS.

THIS PAGE KUGELS are one of the most coveted and pricey of collectible Christmas ornaments. Crafted by German and French artisans, they were made of super-heavy glass. Usually you'll see only balls, in green, silver, or gold. Purple is the rarest; pink-red is almost as obscure. Shapes like the artichoke and grape are especially coveted (and can fetch a few thousand dollars).

OPPOSITE The earliest types of artificial Christmas trees were made of feathers, a style that originated in the nineteenth century. This GOOSE-FEATHER TOPIARY is a lyrical example of the genre. It's decked out with très desirable small-sized kugels in a limited palette.

MOST TYPES OF COLLECTORS HAVE a practical side, whether that's limiting acquisitions to a particular palette (the colorist), confining an obsession to a succinct time of year (the seasonalist), or amassing small items that take up little space (the miniaturist). For the pragmatist, it's not how they collect but what they collect: that is, objects that have a purposeful function. The pragmatist cherishes antique keys, old brooms, nineteenth-century watering cans, vintage eyewear and bottle openers, and other serviceable tools. Although collecting is for many a biological imperative, the act is often viewed as an indulgence; pursuing utilitarian objects is how pragmatists grant themselves permission to gratify that superfluous-seeming urge. Even the most reluctant collectors can talk themselves into just one more corkscrew or galvanized-steel bucket.

Hard to believe a simple tool like a spoon could present such boundless variety. Although highly decorative SPOONS are usually the ones to inspire manic fandom, this collection celebrates the straightlaced beauty of serviceable, unadorned versions. It includes historic and modern iterations—from ladles to teaspoons—in metal, wood, ceramic, bone, plastic, and pressed cardboard.

"Well, I really could use another," the pragmatist thinks, while making a beeline for the cash register.

Of course, once they do submit to that "just one more" impulse, the item is not necessarily pressed into service; "practical" is merely a conceit that enables the purchase. The pragmatist's collection of pitchers may reside in the kitchen, but only one or two will wind up in heavy rotation. The remainder will be showcased in a glass-enclosed vitrine, wrangled into a pleasing composition, or clustered atop a door frame to create a charming decorative accent. Though practicality drives the subject matter, pragmatists are often quite fanciful and inventive in their display practices. They might arrange spare cast-iron baking tins into an unexpectedly chic fireback or hang them salon-style on picture hooks in the dining room. Practicality and creativity go hand in hand.

Another defining trait of the pragmatist is an encyclopedic exploration of their chosen subject. They typically collect large quantities in pursuit of breadth and comprehensiveness. The pragmatist delights in the way different shapes of French curves or bristle brushes speak to different uses. They take an almost academic interest in discerning how formal variations derive from unique (and sometimes obsolete) functions. There are salt spoons and mustard spoons, five o'clock spoons and egg spoons, coffee spoons and soupspoons. Within the pitcher category, there exist creamers, washbasin pitchers, and milk

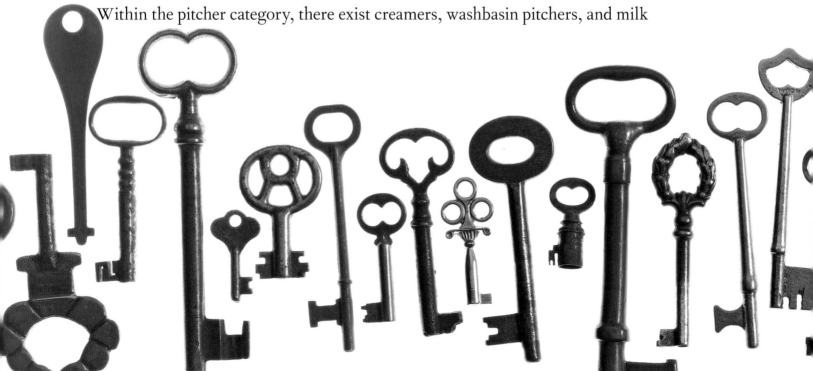

pitchers, among many others. Much intrigue lies in these granular variations within a genre.

The pragmatist finds high artistry in items of utility and necessity. To them, food molds are sculpture, homemade watering cans are folk art, and paint palettes are abstract canvases. They are fascinated by cultures that make a religion of aesthetic purity and economy of design. Pragmatists collect Shaker brooms, hammers crafted by nineteenth-century English toolmakers, and Japanese brushes. They also have a taste for items intended for industrial applications but suited to residential use, such as ceramic lab ware— minimalist, unembellished items designed with use value, not whimsy, in mind. Reframed in a domestic context, these vintage devices look utterly modern.

Although there is an unassuming character to what the pragmatist covets, such items aren't necessarily cheap. Sure, vintage keys can be had for just a few dollars; same with little salt spoons. But curios like eighteenth-century ivory folding rulers may cost thousands of dollars. Their rising value reflects the ever-expanding definition of what is collectible, as well as the timelessness and enduring usefulness of decades- or centuries-old tools that were so smartly designed.

The humble KEY is another age-old tool that tantalizes collectors with its stylistic diversity. This sampling showcases manifold shapes and applications—doors, trunks, lockboxes, cupboards, bookcases.

OPPOSITE **Though born of utility, the workaday pitcher takes on many stylistic guises. The design elements of body, handle, and spout were sculpted and molded into endless silhouettes, with materials spanning the spectrum of metal to glass. This collection of IRONSTONE, STONEWARE, AND MILK-GLASS PITCHERS is unified by color palette—all creams and whites.**

THIS PAGE **A tucked-away hallway was transformed into a paean to pitchers, from stout glazed-ceramic vessels to the rather rarefied GLASS WHIMSY that enjoys pride of place on an accent table. This pragmatist took advantage of unexpected (but practical) display spaces: not only the windowsill but also the ledge atop of the door frame.**

With its clean-lined Bauhaus bearing, vintage INDUSTRIAL LAB WARE looks right at home in the contemporary abode. Most coveted are early twentieth-century examples by Coors, a Colorado-based company that still wholesales to scientific and medical labs. The high-fired ceramic bodies were designed to withstand extreme heat, while the glaze renders the material easy to clean and impervious to chemicals—characteristics that suit the vessels to kitchen applications, too.

Old-school GRADUATED CYLINDERS AND BEAKERS are easy to date: Early versions are free blown and have hand-engraved measurements, while later ones were pressed in a mold and stencil-etched. The shape and size differed depending on the purpose, whether for beauty supplies or medicine; the vessels were often labeled according to use.

OPPOSITE Cast-iron muffin and BAKING MOLDS were often bestowed as gifts-with-purchase to those buying a new stove. Prized for their sculptural look and inventive textural patterns, the molds are also functionally superior: Thinner vintage cast-iron cookware holds and distributes heat better than thicker contemporary versions.

THIS PAGE There are many creative ways to display a collection of BAKING AND MUFFIN PANS, but this idea takes the cake: using a baker's dozen to line a firebox. The concept makes perfect sense, as the cast-iron surfaces reflect the heat into the room and protect the hearth, much like a traditional fireback. The bakeware came in a wide spectrum of geometric designs, from ubiquitous corn husk shapes to less common hearts and rosettes.

THIS PAGE Designed to conceive the utlimate castle-style confection for a big event, these tin LAYER-CAKE PANS can nest inside one another when stored—or create a conversation piece when stacked.

OPPOSITE Food molds were made in many materials, from luxe copper to these more demure tin and aluminum versions by Austrian and German makers. (They are often stamped with the country of origin on the side.) Displayed in a tiered vignette on a side table, these molds look architectural, like modernist pavilions. Above are small JELL-O MOLDS, many created as giveaways.

Pouillot Léon

OPPOSITE French curves and drafting triangles are functional implements with a decorative presence. Each of these was designed for a specific use, like sketching the complex curves of boat hulls. Today, these ENGINEERING TOOLS are usually made of plastic or metal, but vintage versions (as well as superior contemporary ones) were crafted from stable, tight-grained wood such as pear, mahogany, or holly.

THIS PAGE Used in the service of creating paintings, hand-planed WOOD PALETTES—carved from a single piece of wood—are abstract canvases in their own right, dappled with colorful blobs and swooshes of dried paint.

PROPPING CURIOS UP IN A TELESCOPING STYLE FROM LARGE TO SMALL DRAWS ATTENTION TO THEIR CURVACEOUS SILHOUETTES.

OPPOSITE Antique MAKE-DOS AND WHATNOTS have a rich back story, speaking both to the era they were originally made and the date of their later (but still vintage) rehabilitation. Such refurbishment was a necessity in times of scarcity, when cracking a dish meant not being able to replace it with a new one. This porcelain platter was sutured back together with metal staples, a common practice in the eighteenth and nineteenth centuries—and a technique perfected by Chinese artisans.

THIS PAGE This luminous tableau looks like a cluster of MILK-GLASS VOTIVES, but in fact none of the vessels began life as a lighting device. The collection includes cheap diner vases, drinking tumblers, fade-glass vessels, and jars from 1960s make-your-own-yogurt sets.

SO MANY COLLECTING CATEGORIES have a seriousness to them: eighteenth-century Gustavian furniture, old coins, Chinese export porcelain, Murano glass. They *look* like precious antiques and are usually treated as such, displayed with a bit of pomp and occupying an elevated place in the collector's home—and in their mind. In contrast, items coveted by the fantasist are more light-hearted, even a bit absurd; their role is to delight. The fantasist obsesses over examples of out-and-out whimsy: lobster-topped swizzle sticks, needlepoint-covered bricks, a miniature fire truck improbably encased in a narrow-necked glass bottle (however did it get in there?). These items serve no function other than to spark pleasure and tickle the imagination.

There is nothing utilitarian about these GLASS BOTTLES, transformed into display vitrines for handcrafted folk art. Ranging from vehicles to intricate miniature room scenes, the carved follies are sealed inside the glass via equally elaborate stoppers.

The fantasist craves joy, whimsy, and adorableness in their everyday life—the draw is almost Proustian—and finds it in the vintage world. Fantasists surround themselves with frilly tableware, punchy-patterned mid-century linens, and op art clothing. They covet things that transport them to a happier frame of mind—or to fantasy worlds and other eras. Like time machines, the fantasist's collection whisks them straight to the roaring twenties or the disco seventies, harkening back to the unique style of a specific period.

The fantasist is something of an armchair traveler, hankering for state-printed dish towels and old-school silk aviation maps. Vintage travel guides from the nineteenth century are for the most part outdated, no longer serving their intended purpose as information tools. But in a contemporary context they take on a new life as nostalgic documents of a bygone era—the advent of modern leisure travel—and as beautiful objects that conjure exotic locales and inspire a smile.

The fantasist is tickled by items that are unabashedly decorative but that take the form of something utilitarian: beadwork "baskets" that have no bottoms and can't properly hold contents. In the same vein are ersatz hats designed as novelty bookends, spittoons, storage containers, and the like. Even though such items have an overt function, fantasists covet them as pure objets d'art.

Another fixation is seemingly purposeful household tools taken to a wildly ornamental place. Consider a fake book carved out of marble, which serves no other function than to charm. Or a saltshaker shaped like a head of broccoli, more tabletop accent than crafty utensil. And you can stir coffee with an 1890s souvenir spoon, its silver handle carved into a crocodile, but these keepsakes are better relegated to display. Gravitating to genres such as glassware, swizzle sticks, textiles, and doorstops, this strain of fantasist might seem to have a strong pragmatic streak. But there's nothing particularly

practical about clothes brushes mimicking top-hatted gentlemen (especially when they're lined up en masse, like a sales convention, on a mantel). The fantasist doesn't even feign interest in utility; the sole driver is pleasure.

Because the fantasist collects items based on appearance, versus provenance or historical significance, they often dream up inventive ways to show off their wares. They'll arrange pressed-glass cake stands as a sculptural centerpiece on a dining-room table—like a fantasy bakery—or fashion retro dish towels into cute curtains and pillows. The fantasist is also fond of over-the-top installations, fitting out a little loo in full-height shelving to display hundreds of glass bottle whimsies, or utilizing walls, floors, and ceilings as a canvas to showcase prized antique tiles. In this way, fantasists quite literally immerse themselves in an imaginative world of their own making.

Look again: What appears to be the fruits of a shopping trip to the farmers' market is actually a tableau of novelty SALT AND PEPPER SHAKERS—a genre in which form (and artistic license) frequently trumps function.

Treasure hunters will discover all manner of doodads sealed inside GLASS BOTTLES or lightbulbs: birds, boats, furniture, knitty-knotties, room scenes, tassels, god's eyes, Masonic iconography, crucifixes. The product of painstaking workmanship, the mini devices, often scrimshaw carvings, were either partially fabricated inside the bottle or designed so they could be collapsed and re-expanded, like an umbrella, once inserted. Works can generally be dated by the age of the bottle; this fantasist's assortment is primarily nineteenth-century American. Among her most prized finds is a horizontal bottle encasing a hook-and-ladder fire engine. Other gems include a bird tree, weavers working on a double-decker loom, a two-story house with furnished rooms, and a saloon. Although many of these curios were created by anonymous crafters, there are a handful of famous makers whose output is highly coveted, including Warner bottles (at left), elaborate confections that often featured multistory interiors.

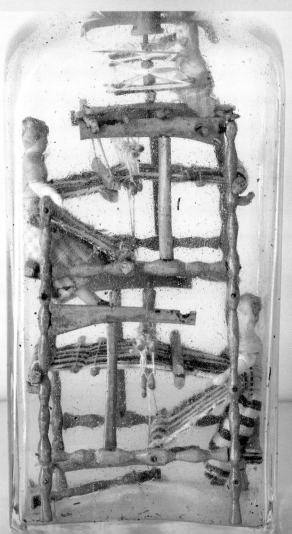

THIS PAGE Pressed glass is pure whimsy. The lyrical shapes were made by a molding process that achieved the exuberance of hand-cut glass at an affordable-for-the-masses price point. (A telling difference: Pressed glass often has visible seams.) With their lace-like forms, these CAKE PLATES make perfect pedestals for similarly sweet confections.

OPPOSITE Eyewear is an accessory that follows the ever-changing tides of fashion; donning them alters the wearer's mood and attitude in a single gesture. Although some people collect just SUNGLASSES or a certain style of SPECS, this particular horde is a timeline of trends, from sixties zany to big-hair eighties to nineties retro.

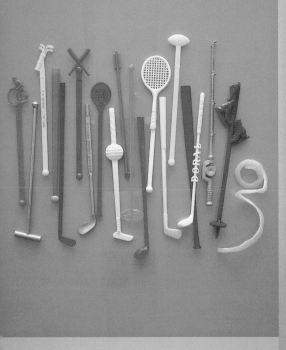
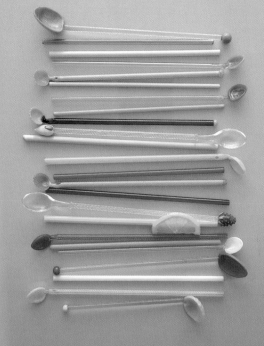

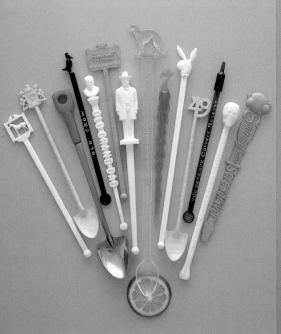
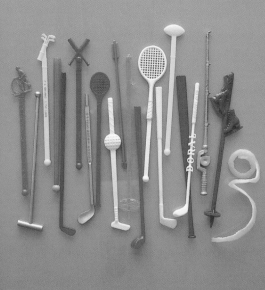

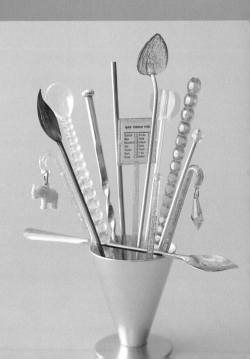

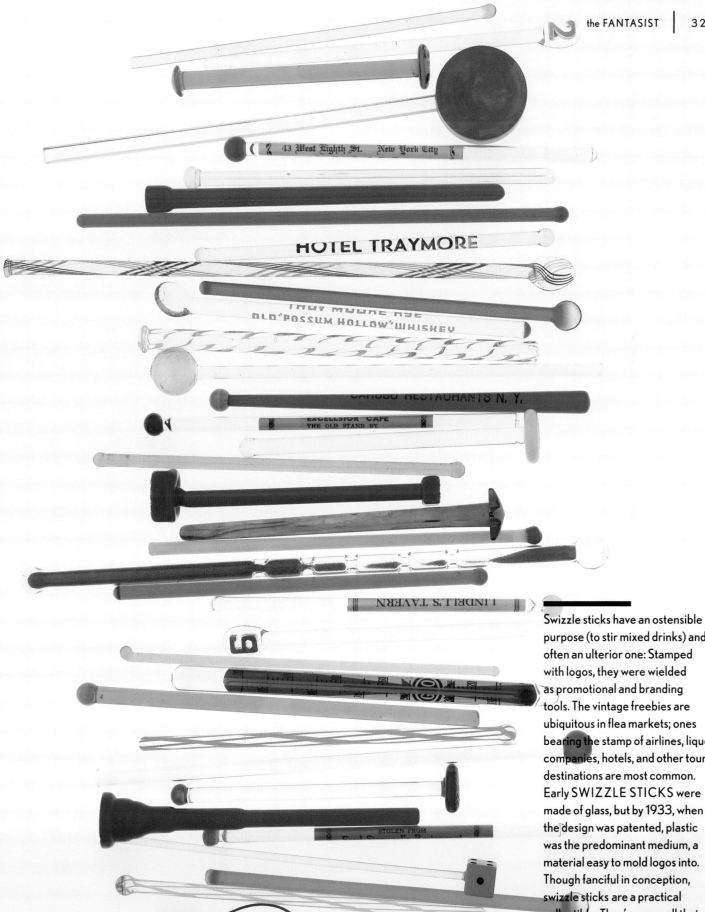

Swizzle sticks have an ostensible purpose (to stir mixed drinks) and often an ulterior one: Stamped with logos, they were wielded as promotional and branding tools. The vintage freebies are ubiquitous in flea markets; ones bearing the stamp of airlines, liquor companies, hotels, and other tourist destinations are most common. Early SWIZZLE STICKS were made of glass, but by 1933, when the design was patented, plastic was the predominant medium, a material easy to mold logos into. Though fanciful in conception, swizzle sticks are a practical collectible: They're so small that even an advanced horde takes up little room.

A bare brick would make a perfectly serviceable doorstop, but wrapping one in a graphic NEEDLEPOINT COZY elevates it from implement to indulgence.

Have abundant wall space to fill and can't afford blue-chip art? A fanciful—and affordable—alternative is to make your own abstract canvases by staple-gunning inexpensive vintage textiles over wooden art stretchers. From afar, this WOOL BLANKET looks just like a painting (and softens acoustics, too).

THIS PAGE Typically made of printed linen or cotton, the retro DISH TOWEL may be a humble houseware, but it's also a major collecting craze. Textile mavens will pay eighty dollars for a rare Tammis Keefe or Vera design, but no-name versions are still very affordable—and the pretty patterns just as precious.

OPPOSITE A roundup of vintage GRAPHIC-PRINT TEXTILES demonstrates the imaginative quality of midcentury design. A plain white cloth would dry dishes just as well, but these flights of fancy made the drudgery of chores imminently more bearable. Other than a few women who became brand names, female home-textile designers toiled in relative obscurity. Though working anonymously, many were exceptionally talented artists, and their diverse output—from dishtowels and hankies to tablecloths—is prized today.

OPPOSITE **Why not liberate spare DISHTOWELS, TABLECLOTHS, AND HANDKERCHIEFS** from the drawer and use them as décor? Stitch them into pillows, collage them into quilts, fashion them into curtains, or laminate one onto a roller shade. These map textiles were made for all the states as well as for regions like the northwest.

THIS PAGE **A little elbow grease** is all it takes to turn a small stash of **VINTAGE MAP TABLECLOTHS AND HANKIES** into a cluster of cushions and throw pillows. You'll often find vintage textiles with stains or frayed edges; simple sewing adaptations can make them serviceable once again and breathe new life into a collection.

The vibrant sheaths and blouses of LILLY PULITZER are perennially popular, coveted for their citrusy hues and prepster patterns. Although the label—started by the eponymous Palm Beach socialite in the 1950s—occasionally re-releases vintage designs, original garments from its 1960s/1970s heyday are quite rare and increasingly collected today. This fantasist covets only women's and children's Lilly clothes.

This vintage clothing dealer and collector pursues men's LILLY BLAZERS; his archive is currently forty strong. (He also collects pants, shirts, and bathing suits.) Although many of his pieces are museum caliber, they're not relegated to display: he regularly wears the mod, mood-lifting leisure wear out and about. Residing in a tropical climate, he's always ready for poolside hangouts.

This fantasist has a thing for quirky craved gentlemen—actually a collection of vintage BAR ACCESSORIES (in the spark plug case at bottom) and dresser-top CLOTHING BRUSHES (on the mantel). Fashioned of hand-carved, hand-painted wood, most were made at the beginning of the twentieth century in Italy or Germany, near the Black Forest where there was a strong tradition of wood carving.

A collection of MAPS adds a worldly touch to a child's bedroom. The decorative treatment extends from the walls to the ceiling, creating an enveloping, cocooning vibe—not to mention an unexpected departure from the usual kid's-room decor staples. It is common to find vintage maps mounted on linen, but ones designed for nautical and aviation use were printed directly on lightweight cloth, generally silk or rayon, which doesn't disintegrate when wet.

ARDET·FORTVNA

This fireplace, one of eighteen in the forty-four-room castle, features a lofty hearth mosaicked in an array of Mercer's **HANDCRAFTED TILES,** made in his neighboring ceramic factory.

Fonthill Castle in Doylestown, Pennsylvania, is the former home of Henry Chapman Mercer, a leader of the American Arts & Crafts movement. A trained archaeologist and anthropologist, Mercer was also a professional ceramist who founded his own tile factory. He collected European prints and decorative ceramic tiles from around the world and lived immersed in his enthusiasms, encrusting every surface of his home with antique tiles from Persia, China, Spain, and Holland as well as contemporary versions of his own design.

He built the home, completed in 1912, specifically to showcase his collections; it's now operated as a museum. Tiles are inset into the castle's floors, vaulted ceilings, and even the base and capitals of the poured-concrete columns. Also visible in the landing is a selection of Mercer's ANTIQUE PRINT collection.

These vintage "books" are all decoys; the collection includes DOORSTOPS, PAPERWEIGHTS, LOVE TOKENS, BOOKENDS, and hollow containers used to hide valuables. Ones crafted of marble or stone are generally solid, while metal and wood versions are typically hollow. This fantasist lives with his collection clustered together like a pile of recent reads on a side table.

FOLLOWING SPREAD Cuff links would seem to be utilitarian, suturing shirt-sleeves together like buttons. But these accessories are pure jewelry, an excuse to add a bit of bling to one's wrist. CUFF LINK design changed over the decades, from loose chains to larger, clasping versions in the 1960s. This fantasist's collection includes a sparkly variety of over-the-top, fashion-forward designs that exude a Rat Pack aura.

The segment of Dixie Highway stretching between Kentucky and Florida was known as Peacock Alley or Bedspread Boulevard, so named for the roadside proprietors who sold handmade textiles to motor tourists. The tufted style of chenille—an attempt to mimic the look of English candlewicking—originated in Evans, Georgia, and grew into a regional cottage industry.

OPPOSITE Made of thin cotton or muslin, vintage HANDMADE CHENILLE wasn't as durable as later commercially woven textiles. Lovingly worn bedding—too threadbare to use, too precious to toss—is ripe for reinvention into a new application. Just stitch salvageable scraps, trims, and cutout motifs into cushions or throw pillows.

THIS PAGE A collection of vintage CHENILLE BEDSPREADS is transformed into a textural decorative treatment. The plush graphic fabric was used to upholster a bedroom wall and outsize headboard, while a geometric element of the pattern was converted into a giant pillow.

An eccentric society figure and self-taught decorator, Henry Davis Sleeper was the father of offbeat but magical color combinations. Sleeper's tour de force was Beauport, his summer residence in Gloucester, Massachusetts. One of the most fanciful rooms was this octagonal dining area. Although the design was grounded in the colonial vernacular, inventive displays of GLASS, WEDGEWOOD, AND TOLE made a surprisingly contemporary statement.

The heyday of the SOUVENIR SPOON CRAZE was 1880 to about 1905, a period when travel became more accessible to middle-class Americans. Tourists would buy these whimsical keepsakes as mementos of a vacation.

THE PHOTO CREDITS

FRONT ENDPAPERS: (from top left) Maria Robledo; Maria Robledo; Vivian Pickles; Dana Gallagher; Dana Gallagher; José Picayo; Jose Picayo; Dana Gallagher; Gentl & Hyers; Vivian Pickles; Maria Robledo; Dana Gallagher; Dana Gallagher; Maria Robledo; Catherine Gratwicke; Maria Robledo; Maria Robledo; Dana Gallagher BACK ENDPAPERS: (from top left) Vivian Pickles; Dana Gallagher; Maria Robledo; Sang An; Maria Robledo; Gentl & Hyers; Maria Robledo; Vivian Pickles; Craig Cutler; Jose Picayo; Maria Robledo; Catherine Gratwicke; Dana Gallagher; Dana Gallagher; Sang An; Dana Gallagher; Jose Picayo; Jose Picayo PAGE 2 GRID: (from top left) Dana Gallagher; Gentl & Hyers; Vivian Pickles; Maria Robledo; Dana Gallagher; Dana Gallagher; Dana Gallagher; Dana Gallagher; Jose Picayo; Gentl & Hyers; Dana Gallagher; Gentl & Hyers; Maria Robledo; Jose Picayo; Catherine Gratwicke; Dana Gallagher

William Abranowicz: 110, 277; **David Allee:** 75; **Sang An:** 34, 54, 55, 133, 138, 154, 196, 197, 244, 251, 268, 288, 289, 326, 327; **Burcu Avsar:** 129, 183; **Christopher Baker:** 212, 213, 308, 309; **Bill Batten:** 74, 254; **Beer Can House, photos courtesy of:** 22, 23; **Rolland Bello:** 161, 162, 163; **Antoine Bootz:** 192, 204, 205, 226, 285, 286; **Andrea Brizzi:** 186, 187; **Anita Calero:** 242, 243, 265; **Craig Cutler:** 278, 283 (top left), 324; **Mauro Davoli:** 184; **Gilles De Chabaneix:** 334; **Pieter Estersohn:** 39, 48, 49, 50, 51, 89, 259, 337; **Sally Gall:** 274, 275; **Dana Gallagher:** 4, 6, 12, 14, 15, 16, 17, 18, 19, 20, 21, 24, 25, 27, 28, 29, 30, 31, 32, 33, 37, 38, 40, 41, 44, 45, 46, 47, 68, 72, 73, 76, 78, 7980, 81, 82, 83, 84, 85, 86, 87, 88, 90, 94, 96, 97, 98, 100, 101, 102, 103, 104, 105, 108, 109, 111, 112, 114, 115, 117, 118, 119, 120, 121, 122, 123, 126, 134, 140, 141, 142, 143, 144, 146, 147, 149, 151, 159, 160, 166, 167, 170, 171, 172, 174, 175, 176, 177, 179, 180, 181, 182, 185, 195, 202, 203, 207, 208, 209, 210, 214, 215, 219, 222, 223, 224, 225, 228, 229, 230, 231, 232, 233, 236, 240, 241, 245, 246, 247, 248, 249, 250, 253, 260, 269, 272, 276, 280, 281, 290, 297, 302, 304, 305, 310, 311, 314, 315, 317, 318, 320, 321, 322, 323, 325, 328, 332, 333, 336, 340, 341, 347, 348;

Gentl & Hyers: 106, 107, 132, 158, 282, 283 (bottom right), 293, 294, 295, 296, 306, 307, 313; **Catherine Gratwicke:** 56, 57; **Troy House:** 298, 299; **Lisa Hubbard:** 42, 43; **Ditte Isager:** 92, 93; **Sam Kaufman Gallery:** 168, 169; **Eric Kvatek:** 77; **David Mann:** Fritz Karch author photo; **Toni Meneguzzo:** 135; **James Mollison for *COLORS* issue 79:** 26; **Amy Neunsinger:** 330; **Victoria Pearson:** 155, 267/Getty Images, 300, 301/Getty Images, 344, 345; **Eric Piasecki:** 53, 136, 137, 139, 164, 211, 273, 346, Rebecca Robertson author photo; **Jose Picayo:** 58, 59, 130, 145, 150, 152, 165, 178, 188, 189, 196, 238, 287, 312, 335; **Vivian Pickles:** 52, 70, 71, 91, 95, 124, 125, 234, 235, 252, 258, 284, 331, 342, 343; **Maria Robledo:** 113, 156, 157, 262, 264, 283 (bottom left), 316; **Scott & Zoe:** 292; **Victor Schrager:** 257, 271; **Mark Seelen:** 60, 64, 65, 66, 67; **Anson Smart:** 270; **Martin Solyst:** 148; **Joanne Tinker, courtesy of Woolff Gallery, London:** 116; **Jonny Valiant:** 329; **Mikkel Vang:** 198, 199; **Jens Veerbeck for *COLORS* issue 79:** 190, 191; **Deidi Von Schaewen:** 11; **Bjorn Wallander:** 206, 261, 263, 266, 338, 339; **Mark Weiss:** 200, 201; **Anna Williams:** 216, 220, 221, 227, 291

VINTAGE CAMERAS were produced in all sizes, formats, and functions, but even within one micro-category—inexpensive tourist point-and-shoots—there were differences in body shape, flash configuration, and button style. Most in this collection are mid-century designs by Kodak; their compact, lightweight forms were ideal for tucking into luggage or toting around while on vacation.

THE ACKNOWLEDGMENTS

We would like to thank all the amateur and professional collectors, crafters, scavengers, artists, photographers, art directors, stylists, and antique and junk shop dealers and owners for their generosity, and for sharing their always-impressive and often-unique personal worlds, passions, and energies to make our book possible.

William Abranowicz
Liz Adler
Larry Becker
Jonathan Bee
Kyle Bitters
Bill Blass
Bonnet House Museum & Gardens
Lisa Congdon
Roger Crowley
Jill Dienst
James Dunlinson
Patti Gaal-Holmes
Amy P. Goldman
Walter and Ise Gropius
Jason Hamilton
Katie Hatch
Nancy Heckler
Scott Horne
Kent Hunter
Andrea Karras
Sam Kaufman
Hugo Kohnhorst
Cary Leibowitz
Simon Lince

Nancy Lorenz
David Mann
Marcie McGoldrick
Jeff McKay
Henry Chapman Mercer
Ellen Morrissey
Museo Guatelli
John Milkovisch
Larry and Debbie Onie
Eric Pike
Andrea and Charles Rabinovitch
Patricia Robertson
Carlos Salgado
Sue Sheen
Henry Davis Sleeper
Silke Stoddard
Joanne Tinker, courtesy of Woolff Gallery
Alistair Turnbull
Keni Valenti
Jens Veerbeck
Vizcaya Museum & Gardens
Allison, JP, and Piper Williams
Valerie and Matthew Young

Dana Gallagher, our photographer and longtime friend: we could not have done this book without you, your team, and your amazing talent! Our writer, Jen Renzi: you brought our words to life on the page. Thank you for being an amazing collaborator and a brilliant foil to our nuttiness and disorder. Our agents, David Kuhn and Nicole Tourtelot: for your vision. The Abrams team: Deborah Aaronson, Deb Wood, Rebecca Kaplan, Meg Parsont—for your enthusiasm, talent, and wisdom. Thank you to the other photographers whose incredible work is included in this book. Yvette Gonzales: for all of your help making this book happen. Ellen Morrissey: for your brilliance. Martha Stewart: for giving collecting a forum, and for being an inspiration to us both. All our colleagues at *Martha Stewart Living*: editors, stylists, art directors, and creative partners whose work is included in this book.

THE DEDICATION

From Rebecca Robertson

Marco and Luca: you are my champions, my inspiration, and my loves. Mom and Dad: thank you for instilling in me a love of all things old, broken, and beautiful and for being my pillars. Will Schwalbe: for your (many) words of wisdom. My family and friends: thank you ALL for your love and support (and for keeping me sane). Fritz, my co-author: you inspire me with your stupendous talent and unfailing kindness and wit.

From Fritz Karch

I dedicate this book to the mentors, relatives, relations, and friends who have encouraged and collaborated in many of my most unconventional and impractical impulses and ideas. I must thank some of them by name, especially David Mann, David and Betty Mcgrail, Joel Mathieson, Robert Kinnaman, Paula Rubinstein, Janet West, John Derian, Joan Pope, and Andrea Karras. Most of all to Rebecca Robertson, the better half of all my thoughts, efforts, instincts, actions, and impulses. She has made most things possible. Much thanks.

Anyone we may have inadvertently left off this list—please forgive us—and contact us so we can update our book website and any subsequent versions of the book.

Editor: Rebecca Kaplan
Designer: Deb Wood
Production Manager: Denise LaCongo

Library of Congress Control Number:
2014930720

ISBN: 978-1-4197-1395-8

Printed and bound in the United States
10 9 8 7 6 5 4 3 2 1

Abrams books are available at special discounts when
purchased in quantity for premiums and promotions
as well as fundraising or educational use. Special
editions can also be created to specification. For
details, contact specialsales@abramsbooks.com
or the address below.

THE ART OF BOOKS SINCE 1949

115 WEST 18TH STREET
NEW YORK, NY 10011
WWW.ABRAMSBOOKS.COM